Teen Challenge radically change  off the streets with an addiction many different rehab programs, was the emphasis on the gospel and the power of the Holy Spirit. In 2009 I was delivered from addiction because of the message of Jesus Christ and the baptism of the Holy Spirit. Today, I lead an evangelistic ministry that helps to reach the lost. Our ministry is deeply inspired by the founding accounts of Teen Challenge as recorded in the book *The Cross and the Switchblade*. Pastor Don Wilkerson's message is essential to ensure that Teen Challenge does not fall into the tragic trap of "mission drift" that many organizations fall into after being in existence for an extended period of time. May this book challenge you and encourage you to keep Christ as the focus.

—Andrew Chalmers

Take the City Inc., Founder and Director

A bold, passionate, and powerful plea to the ministry Don Wilkerson co-founded, to keep the cross central to the story of *The Cross and the Switchblade*. This book exposes the subtle and dangerous ways many once vibrant and gospel-centered ministries have drifted away from the original intent and purpose they were founded on and succumbed to the venom of secularization to raise money and achieve worldly credibility. In this insightful and well-written book, Pastor Don is fighting for the vision he and his brother David Wilkerson had for Teen Challenge over 60 years ago, not to be a rehab but to be a church for the least and the lost of society. I stand with him in his effort to preserve the gospel integrity of this ministry. This book is a must-read for anyone who loves and supports Teen Challenge or is involved in Christian ministry of any kind.

—Joshua West
Pastor of Sonrise Adult & Teen Challenge
and author of *Hard Sayings: Reconciling the Cost
of Discipleship and the American Dream*

I have worked alongside Don Wilkerson in two different seasons of my life. The first was when I was the Prayer Pastor at Times Square Church, and Pastor Don was one of the three leading pastors. The second has been the blessing of serving at Brooklyn Teen Challenge as the Campus Pastor. So I can speak as one who has had the blessing of hearing him preach once a week for six years and then daily working with him at Brooklyn Teen Challenge. It's been said that working in a drug rehab program is so intense that each year is like five years of working in a regular church. For Pastor Don working for decades at Teen Challenge, does this mean he's as experienced as Methuselah? I would rather say that he has the wisdom of Solomon when it comes to Teen Challenge issues. Will Teen Challenge as a whole heed his loving and wise and weather-worn warnings? I certainly hope so. This book deserves a place at conference table discussions in all Teen Challenge centers and faith-based ministries.

—Pastor Charles Simpson
Brooklyn Teen Challenge and The Oasis Center, Queens

Jonathan —

KEEPING

THE

CROSS

CENTRAL

Thank you for staying mission true!

DON WILKERSON

Don Wilkerson

BRIDGE LOGOS

Newberry, FL 32669

Bridge-Logos
Newberry, FL 32669

Keeping the Cross Central:
The Faith-Based Legacy of Teen Challenge
by Don Wilkerson

Printed in the United States of America

Library of Congress Catalog Card Number: 2021930260

International Standard Book Number: 978-1-61036-259-7

Cover/Interior design by Kent Jensen | knail.com

Cover background vector created by Harryarts | www.freepik.com

Edited by Lynn Copeland

To my wife, Cindy,
and my children, Kristy, Todd, and Julie:
You never wavered in encouraging me to stay "mission true"
to the original vision of Teen Challenge.

CONTENTS

Foreword *by Dr. Michael L. Brown* ix

Introduction xiii

1. Sounding the Trumpet 1
2. Keeping the Cross Central to the Story 7
3. Generation Next 13
4. We Are Not Professionals 19
5. Called or Hired 25
6. Love Needs an Address 31
7. It's Not Rehab 37
8. Getting to the Root 45
9. The Coin in the Fish's Mouth 53
10. To Whom Honor Is Due 59
11. The Board of Correction 65
12. We've Come This Far by Faith 75
13. The Gospel on Day One 81

Afterword 87

Notes 91

FOREWORD

When I think of Don Wilkerson, I think of an unflappable man of God, always steady, always full of wisdom, always with a smile. But in this book, I see a different side to my dear old friend. He is burdened and concerned. He carries real grief and brings a heavy warning, sounding the alarm. He is jealous for a holy legacy. He does not want to see the cross removed from its central place in the Teen Challenge ministry. Without that central focus, the whole ministry collapses from within.

I remember watching *The Cross and the Switchblade* for the first time while still a teenager, freshly delivered from heavy drug use (including heroin) at the age of sixteen in 1971. We actually showed the movie one night in our little Pentecostal congregation in Queens, New York, and I was deeply stirred after watching it, as if confronted afresh with the amazing grace of the Lord. What an amazing story and what an incredible witness.

About twenty years later, while preaching regularly at Times Square Church for David and Don Wilkerson, I read *The*

Cross and the Switchblade book for the first time. Once again, I was stirred and challenged. What faith. What obedience. What courage. What divine backing. What a Savior!

It was that same divine backing that seemed to accompany David and Don in the ministry work they continued to do, from the powerful conversions that took place every week at Times Square Church to the worldwide spread of Teen Challenge centers. It was the work of the Spirit, and no one could deny that.

A few years later, in 1996, I began working side by side with Evangelist Steve Hill in the Brownsville Revival, where the crowds would form daily at 6:00 a.m. outside the doors of an Assembly of God church building. They were waiting for the service to start at 7:00 p.m., thirteen hours later. God used Steve to win countless thousands of souls to Jesus, and he would often share his personal testimony, which included being a graduate of Teen Challenge himself.

Over the years, leading different ministry schools, we had quite a few Teen Challenge graduates enroll as students, and they often stood out for their depth of devotion to the Lord. They were truly delivered, they were deeply grateful, and they were serious disciples. They knew the sin and darkness in which they once walked, and they now wanted to give their lives to Jesus as deeply as they once gave their lives to the devil.

As I learned more about Teen Challenge centers worldwide, I was thrilled to hear of the ongoing success of the work, with a large percentage of graduates continuing to live drug-free lives. How different this was from the government-sponsored programs, as well-intentioned as they might be. These secular programs were more of a revolving door for addicts than a place of transformation. But what else could we expect? They were devoid of the power of God.

That's why I was so distressed to receive a call from Don telling me about the mission drift within a growing number of Teen Challenge centers in America, as they justified leaving out the cross as long as they could receive government funding. The gospel was now rendered an option rather than a requirement during an entry-level program, all in order to receive monetary help from Uncle Sam. But at what cost?

In that light, I strongly encourage every lover of the Teen Challenge ministry—every grad, every worker and leader, every supporter, every board member—to read this important book carefully. Not only will it bring a powerful caution and corrective to those who are straying, but it will point all of us back to the cross in our own lives. The stories, quotes, and lessons that follow will inspire and edify and challenge.

When illustrating the danger of mission drift, I have sometimes painted this picture. Let's say I feel called to speak to the nation on radio, preaching a message of repentance and revival, but I'm only on twenty-five stations. A PR agent reaches out to me, telling me that if I will emphasize my own personal health transformation and weight loss, I can be on five hundred stations rather than twenty-five. Then, once I build my audience, I can get back to preaching repentance and revival.

Of course, it doesn't work like that, since the audience I will have built across the country will not be interested in the message of holiness and visitation. They want to hear about fitness! In the same way, if we have a vision from the Spirit that we try to advance in the flesh, after which we bring in the Spirit, it will not work.

It is my prayer that God will use this book to bring every single Teen Challenge center that has strayed back to its original mission, calling, and anointing, and that He would supernaturally reinforce all those which are standing strong. May we take heed to the words of this seasoned man of God. May we all look back to the cross.

—Dr. Michael L. Brown
Host of the Line of Fire radio broadcast,
author of *Jezebel's War with America*

INTRODUCTION

One of the primary purposes of this book is to examine the roots of the Teen Challenge ministry to see if today it is ministering as effectively to those with life-controlling problems as it has been from the beginning. Is the cross still central to the story of *The Cross and the Switchblade*?

The Cross and the Switchblade tells about the origin of the ministry of Teen Challenge that my brother, David Wilkerson, founded. I am considered a cofounder. The ministry began reaching gang members in the early 1960s, but then the gangs started using drugs, mainly heroin, and we changed our focus to provide a place where addicts could come and get the "monkey off their back," as they described their addiction at the time.

If you have not read the bestselling *The Cross and the Switchblade*, which shares the story of how Teen Challenge began, you might want to read it along with this book. In the more than fifty years since its publication, this dramatic account has inspired over 15 million readers and, I trust, will inspire you too. I also encourage you to read a more recent book entitled *Giving Hope an Address,* which focuses on the family story and legacy of Teen Challenge. Teen Challenge—has grown from the first center in Brooklyn, New York, to over 1,400 programs in 129 countries, helping addicts find freedom from their addiction. Today, Teen Challenge is also called Adult and Teen Challenge (ATC) to better reflect the populations they serve. For the purposes of this book, I will primarily keep to the original name of Teen Challenge, even though both names are interchangeable.

As the TC cofounder—and the founder in 1995 of Global Teen Challenge, which launched the ministry worldwide—I have had the joy of witnessing firsthand how the "Jesus factor" has changed so many lives trapped in addiction. The success has resulted from the ministry remaining exclusively faith-focused, Bible-based, and Christ-centered for over sixty years.

At this writing I have just officially retired from Brooklyn Teen Challenge. I have served nearly sixty years in the Teen Challenge ministry as executive director of Brooklyn Teen Challenge as well as the founder of Global Teen Challenge. What I share on these pages is from my heart about a ministry to which I have given my entire adult life.

In recent years, some Adult and Teen Challenge centers have opened a short-term (thirty- to ninety-day) program that is government-funded. This means prayer must be limited, and the message of the cross cannot be the focus of the program. Some justify this option in order to help more people battling addiction, and because clients can voluntarily attend chapel services in the traditional, long-term, and faith-based program. The hope is that at the end of the short-term (non-faith-based) stay, the client will choose to transition into the program's long-term, faith-based phase. However, to date, there are no viable statistics of how many do transition, and out of those who do, how many go on to complete the discipleship-based program.

So, I write this book for two primary reasons:

1. To remind those who work in Adult and Teen Challenge of who we are—of the necessity of keeping the message of the cross of Christ and His resurrection power central in transforming those with life-controlling problems.
2. To ensure that TC remains exclusively faith-based and true to its mission. (There is ample evidence that organizations reaching five to six decades of ministry might begin to drift from the founder's vision.)

A book that has impacted me, and which I will quote throughout these pages, is titled *Mission Drift* by Peter Greer and Chris Horst. The subtitle is "The Unspoken Crisis Facing Leaders, Charities, and Churches." The authors advocate that organizations and ministries that are founded as faith-based and remain faith-focused be defined as mission true. They define mission true organizations as those that "know why they exist and protect their core at all costs. They remain faithful to what they believe God has entrusted them to do."[1]

My greater purpose in writing this is to prevent the ministry I have spent my life serving from going the way of Harvard, Yale, and Princeton. These institutions, which were established to train ministers for evangelical ministry, today have drifted as far away from that founding as the east is from the west. My fervent hope is that Teen Challenge will protect its core identity and have eyes of faith like Hezekiah: "With him is an arm of flesh; but with us is the LORD our God, to help us fight our battles" (2 Chronicles 32:8).

ONE

SOUNDING THE TRUMPET

"Indeed it came to pass, when the trumpeters and singers were as one,...praising and thanking the LORD,...the glory of the LORD filled the house..."

—2 Chronicles 5:13,14

Can a *mission drift* happen to Teen Challenge?

No ministry or Christian organization is immune from drifting from its roots. The biggest test for church and parachurch organizations will be determining the sources to which they will look for financial help. Will it be God or mammon?

In their book *Mission Drift*, Greer and Horst state this drift most always begins with the choice of the board of directors:

If the Christian distinctiveness of your organization is something you desire to protect, you cannot budge on the character and caliber of your board. If you go back to the stories of Harvard, Yale, ChildFund, the Y [YMCA], the Pew Trusts, and the many others we found in our research, poor board selection and governance was always one of the driving causes of drift.

If the board isn't composed of folks who live out the values of the organization they lead, the organization will drift. The organization will secularize. It will only be a matter of time.[2]

Has that time come for Teen Challenge?

If the board moves away from the founder's vision, the motivation is typically to receive secular or government funding, even though those who do this try to put a positive spin on their reasons.

There is, in many church and parachurch organizations, what I call "bait and switch." The *bait* can be an advertised method of outreach that addresses a real human need. But the *switch* can be a total departure from the original mission of the organization. In the case of Teen Challenge, this would be like changing our story to be *The Bait and the Switch Blade*. It is unconscionable that any Teen Challenge center would use the successful reputation of sixty-plus years of the faith-based ministry to open a non-faith-based program, where you cannot speak of the name of Jesus, have prayer and worship, or offer biblical counsel.

Andy Crouch, former Executive Director of *Christianity Today*, writes the following in the introduction to *Mission Drift*:

Money plays a key role [in mission drift]…, you cannot understand the secularization of American colleges and universities without understanding the role of the [money factor]. There is also the simple failure to pay attention at crucial moments, such as the selection of board members or the words we use to describe ourselves and our cause to diverse audiences. *Most of all there is the scandal of the Gospel, which constantly calls all human beings and human institutions to repentance and transformation rather than accommodation and self-preservation.*[3] (emphasis added)

The only way to keep Teen Challenge from mission drift, and prevent a departure from the gospel principles it was founded upon, is to keep the cross of Jesus Christ front and center in every phase of the program. My prayer is that God saves us from the secularization of a ministry that was and is God-ordained to help change lives through the message of the cross of Jesus Christ. After all, we don't stand merely on what we do; we stand on the finished work of the cross. First Corinthians 1:18 reminds us that the message of the cross is "the power of God." I am pleased to write that an overwhelming majority of Teen Challenge programs remain faithful to the founding vision. A few have added a pre-entry program that is not faith-based, but the goal is to move those clients to the traditional program. Whether this opens the door to the secularizing of some TC programs, only time will tell. *Keeping the Cross Central* is written to exhort Adult and Teen Challenge centers around the world to maintain the Christ-centered, Bible-based, Spirit-led ministry that has had so much success in witnessing countless lives changed.

Historically, ministries often veer off course from being exclusively faith-based and Christ-centered when new leadership takes control and seeks help—financially and in other ways—from secular partnerships.

I want to make it clear, as previously stated, that the majority of Adult and Teen Challenge centers remain exclusively faith-based and do not take government funds in a way that requires them to be silent about the gospel message. However, some TC centers are operating a short-term government program under a separate name and separate corporation. Yet they still publicly use the Teen Challenge name as if the faith-based part of the ministry and the non-faith-based part are one component. Many of them operate in the same facilities once used exclusively for the traditional faith-based program. I question the ethics of this as donors contributed funds for those faith-based buildings, and I doubt that many would condone the change in usage of the dormitories and homes.

You may think it's fine that a ministry operating for years as exclusively faith-based also has a short-term, non-faith-based program. Perhaps you feel the proximity to the traditional TC program justifies it, or that it is another path to help opioid addicts. I respect that even though it raises my concerns. The only way a ministry can be *mission true* is for every member to be firmly committed to maintaining the message of the cross as the central component throughout the organization, from the board of directors to the CEO, and every staff member—cooks, teachers, pastors, maintenance workers, and counselors. The apostle Paul could not have said it more clearly: "For Christ did not send me to baptize, but to preach the gospel, not with wisdom of words, lest the cross of Christ should be made of no effect" (1 Corinthians 1:17).

Today in the field of drug treatment, there is what I call the gospel of the medical cure, the gospel of therapy and psychology, and the gospel of the Twelve Steps, which is good as far as it goes—but it does not go far enough. Far enough is found at the cross of Jesus Christ.

I am not writing this to harm Teen Challenge but to fully unite it behind the cross. More important than just writing about what we should *not be* is to remind us all of what we *should be*. Teen Challenge is meant to be an exclusively faith-based, Christ-centered, and biblically-based ministry. Its primary goal isn't simply to end addiction but to lead those who enter any TC program to the One who breaks the chains of addiction once and for all and who offers eternal life. This is my call: to encourage you to remember who we are, who we have been, and who and what we need to be going forward. I am not a whistleblower but a trumpeter.

If the *cross* and everything it stands for is removed from the Teen Challenge ministry, then all that will remain is the *switchblade.* In other words, if this "new way'" continues, it may very well be the end of Teen Challenge as it has been known since day one—consistently offering salvation in Jesus Christ and changing lives for over sixty years. I pray that all of us in Teen Challenge will heed Joel's prophecy: "Blow the trumpet in Zion, consecrate a fast, call a sacred assembly;…Let the priests, who minister to the LORD, weep between the porch and the altar" (Joel 2:15,17). I can tell you that there are a host of Teen Challenge leaders and staff who are doing this very thing.

There were two reasons for the sounding of the trumpet in the Old Testament. One was a call to worship, and the other was a gathering for war. This book is a call for both. Let worship be centered on the cross, and let spiritual warfare in overcoming addiction point to Christ and the cross as the only lasting cure.

My brother and I never intended Teen Challenge to become merely a drug-addiction treatment center, but a discipleship program for those who are or were addicts. The former deals with primarily the addiction *problem*; the latter provides the solution in Jesus Christ the moment an addict enters the doors and enrolls in Teen Challenge.

TWO

KEEPING THE CROSS CENTRAL TO THE STORY

"I wish that our ministry—that mine especially—might be tied and tethered to the cross. I would have no other subject to set before you but Jesus only."

—Charles H. Spurgeon

It is a significant challenge to stay on the path of the founder's vision for a God-ordained ministry. One needs to know only the history of the founding of Harvard and Yale universities to understand how mission drift can happen. Historically the drift starts slowly, but by the end of a few decades, the institution has devolved into one with a completely different set of values and an entirely new mission statement.

In the Bible, what would become the nation of Israel began to drift in its infancy when a new generation arose who "did not know the LORD," the God of Abraham, Isaac, and Jacob (Judges 2:10). For over six decades, I have watched Teen Challenge, for the most part, keep the cross of Christ as the cornerstone to the mission of helping addicts overcome their addiction. But this is not without its challenges.

In its founding days, Teen Challenge was called Teen-Age Evangelism. David Wilkerson would say to the first outreach workers (young people from churches or Bible school students) that "God chooses the foolish and weak things of the world to confound the wise and the mighty" (see 1 Corinthians 1:27). From this biblical definition, we gained strength in knowing who we were and in doing what we felt God calling us to do. We were not experts in the field of addiction—not medically or psychologically trained—but rather were a group of leaders and workers, or nobodies. Simply put, we were "foolish things" armed only with our belief in the cross and salvation of Jesus Christ. On the streets of New York City, we shared about the person, the "Somebody," who could change anybody—whether gang member or drug addict. Though we were not trained experts in the causes of addiction or its effect on the abuser, we were skilled when it came to sharing the gospel of salvation and deliverance.

David Wilkerson often shared the following basic message of hope with addicts in open-air street meetings in some of the very first Teen Challenge outreaches during our early days:

God is the only one who can cure you! Nothing is impossible with God... You must believe that the Bible is the Word of

God and that it is true. When you know the truth, the truth will set you free. The Bible makes you this promise: if you confess Him as your Savior—He will make you into a new person.[4]

The message of hope to all sinners has not changed in over two thousand years, nor, indeed, the last sixty years since Teen Challenge's founding. I have witnessed this same message changing the lives of troubled youth, gang members, drug and alcohol abusers, prostitutes, and others worldwide. May the message stay the same until Jesus Christ returns.

The uniqueness of Teen Challenge was, and hopefully always will be, that it is a place where the gospel is out front, not hidden, camouflaged, or watered down to please donors. Nor is it an organization where individual directors are chosen for the board because of their political or financial power or because they agree with a new direction for the organization.

Drifting from the simplicity of the gospel is a slippery slope, which surprisingly is happening even to veteran leaders of an organization. They can get burned out on budget shortfalls and the tiresome nickel-and-dime methods of fundraising. Many a good man or woman of God has unwittingly drifted from their organization's first calling by agreeing to non-faith-based practices to qualify for funds from secular sources.

One Teen Challenge leader has replaced discipleship with non-discipleship programming in the initial stages of their residential program, and thus reaps a vast financial income and boasts of that income. Although parts of the ministry remain faith-based in practice, my response is that this is not a testimony but an indictment against the entire Teen Challenge ministry.

This is not to say that outsiders from the family of faith cannot be helpful through financial or other contributions to an organization. In my brother's early days of establishing our ministry, a wise businessman suggested that nonbelievers or nominal Christians might be turned off by the word "evangelism" in the original name of the organization. Thus, David renamed our ministry from Teen-Age Evangelism to Teen Challenge, *but this did not affect the ministry's Christ-centered purpose.*

It is crucial to make sure that whatever advice, donations, or influences are offered by an outside contributor, including a government entity (especially a government entity), be evaluated regarding whether it helps a ministry to stay on, or stray from, its mission.

Some ways that an organization can keep being *mission true* and not drift from the founder's original vision are:

- Measure outcomes not by financial metrics, but by whether the goal of the transformation of those served remains central to its purpose.
- Ensure that every staff member and worker in any position of the organization has a vibrant relationship with Jesus Christ.
- Make sure that the mission and vision statements are entirely in operation in every part and division of the ministry, without exception.
- Hold both the gospel message and the gospel methods to biblical standards. A. W. Tozer writes: "The cross stands high above the opinions of men and to that cross all opinions come must at last for judgment."[5]

I am emphatic that any Teen Challenge worthy of its name present the gospel of Jesus Christ *on day one* as a student enters the program. Matthew West has a song that I love titled "Day One." A few of its lyrics are: "It's day one of the rest of my life.... I'm marching on to the beat of a brand new drum. Yeah, here I come, the future has begun."[6] I might add the future begins at the cross, which in the words of an old hymn is where "I first saw the light, and the burden of my heart rolled away."[7]

The fact is that any organization that purports to be evangelistic yet receives government funds—and therefore cannot preach the gospel from day one or any other day in the government-funded part of the program—is experiencing *mission drift*.

In the early days of Teen Challenge, we sang out of donated hymnals during chapel service. As I recall those days, I laugh when I think of the hardcore heroin addicts singing the traditional church hymns. Their favorite was "There's Power in the Blood." Why that particular hymn? Because they knew the destructive power of a substance going through their veins, promising them heaven but delivering hell. There is the promise of another higher and greater power, as the hymn asks: "Would you be free from the burden of sin?"[8] The promise of the gospel message was and is still found in Christ's shed blood on the cross. That promise ought to serve as the DNA of Teen Challenge: **D**o **N**ot **A**lter the message that "there's power in the blood" of Christ to transform anyone.

Charles Spurgeon, the great English preacher in the 1800s, writes the following about the cross:

This is the greatest sight you will ever see. Son of God and Son of Man, there He hangs, bearing pain unutterable, the just for the unjust, to bring us to God. Oh, the glory of the sight...There is no place like Calvary for creating confidence. The air of that sacred hill brings health to trembling faith.[9]

What are some of the things that help keep a ministry centered on the cross of Christ? We'll cover that in more detail in the next chapter.

THREE

GENERATION NEXT

"Which we have heard and known, and our fathers have
told us. We will not hide them from their children,
telling to the generation to come the praises of the LORD, *and*
His strength and His wonderful works that He has done."

—Psalm 78:3,4

While seeking to keep the ministry I have served exclusively faith-focused, Bible-based, and Christ-centered, I have been blessed to have many leaders in Teen Challenge contact me to say they will continue to model their centers after David Wilkerson's original vision in *The Cross and the Switchblade.* I am nearing the end of my career, but I have the blessed assurance that this ministry will stay *mission true* through what I call "Generation Next."

Just as Allstate Insurance promises their customers that they will be "in good hands," so most of the current leadership of Adult and Teen Challenge programs do not want to sell out financially but to continue to be "sold out" to ministering to the souls of our clients/students in the program. The term "clients" is a clinical term used only by those who receive government funding. Teen Challenge has always called our residents "students" to denote they are in a learning program being taught to be disciples of Jesus Christ.

When the children of Israel occupied the Promised Land, there was a period when "the people served the LORD all the days of Joshua, and all the days of the elders who outlived Joshua, who had seen all the great works of the LORD..." (Judges 2:7). Those elders/leaders today are "Generation Next." Such a generation is now in place in Teen Challenge, with the exception of those wanting to go in a different direction. My faith is in the next generation.

Greer and Horst write in *Mission Drift*: "Too often, the passions of the first generation become the preferences of the second generation and are irrelevant to the third generation."[10] I am witnessing some of those of the first generation losing their passion for this ministry to be exclusively faith-based. But some of the steadfast ones are graduates of the program. Paul Burke, who served under me at Brooklyn Teen Challenge and is now its Executive Director, is one of them. He is a fourteen-year graduate of Long Island Teen Challenge. He came to know Christ under Willie Ramos, now Executive Director of New York State Adult and Teen Challenge. Ramos is a twenty-year graduate from both Brooklyn and Long Island Teen Challenge. I consider both Ramos and Burke to be models of what I see in scores of leaders in this ministry worldwide—they have the DNA of Teen Challenge firmly planted within them. They are my heroes.

I see our steadfast graduate leaders as examples of the indigenous principle in missions work. Indigenous means "originating or occurring naturally [in a place]; native."[11] When missionaries go to an unevangelized area of the world, they often leave behind a Christian church of converts from that culture and language. This is the indigenous principle. The unconverted come to Christ, and two things happen. First, they are discipled, and then they are trained to evangelize their own people. Some go on to become pastors, teachers, etc., and congregations are raised up, as was the example in the book of Acts. Jewish converts reached Jews and then Gentiles. Gentile converts, in turn, then reached the lost Gentiles, and so on. Such has been the way of our Christian faith since the days of the early church.

Although American missionaries may be sent to make converts in various countries, among other races or ethnicities, the most effective and lasting discipleship happens indigenously. Africans reach Africans. Asians reach Asians. Latins reach Latins.

The ministry focus of Teen Challenge is to raise up those saved in a subculture to become missionaries to that same subculture. Today there are countless ex-addicts reaching addicted populations. Ex-prisoners are missionaries to those in prison, and the formerly homeless are now missionaries on the streets to the homeless. In Teen Challenge, there is now an army of Christian soldiers using the weapons of faith to make war on drugs and rescue addicts from their enslavement.

There are others who have been raised in this ministry as sons or daughters (or a brother, in my case) of directors and are called to it. They too have the DNA of Teen Challenge birthed in them from the womb, a spiritual upbringing where as a matter of daily living they saw the wonders of the cross transforming outcasts into new creations in Christ Jesus (2 Corinthians 5:17). They certainly feel no less the call to serve as cross-carriers and cross-cultural missionaries to those with life-controlling problems.

This indigenous principle has happened naturally over the past six decades in Teen Challenge. Those addicted to drugs and alcohol get saved and delivered, discipled, and trained. Many of those converts are evangelists, pastors, leaders, Teen Challenge executive directors, teachers, biblical counselors, workers, and faithful members of local churches. Some even serve as board members in the same Teen Challenge program that helped lift them out of their pit. I trust them to carry out the original purpose of Teen Challenge more than anyone else. There are also numerous graduates who operate programs similar to Teen Challenge but under different names. They too are staying the course and not drifting away from the cross.

Lives that have been transformed through Adult and Teen Challenge are living testimonies of the gospel legacy of the ministry. Compromise that aspect, and we become just another rehab program. Every successful graduate validates the original purpose of our founding. They are modern miracles of the eternal vision of the Lord Jesus Christ and the foundation of the church. They are the life-size "signs and wonders" with hands, feet, hearts, and bodies—living proof of the original Teen Challenge vision. This was recently confirmed in several posts on my Facebook page from TC graduates. Here are a few comments about the possibility of *mission drift* and Teen Challenge not remaining true to its original vision:

- "The only reason TC worked for me was that it wasn't a watered-down, government-funded program. It spoke God's truth in love, something the secular [program] is incapable of."
- "If they [the TC centers] change their methods, they should change their name."
- "Please don't kick the Word of God and Jesus out of TC. If Teen Challenge becomes secularized, the very essence of what TC is will cease to be. I graduated from TC and encountered God there. I left my old life and haven't looked back."
- "Since you can't ever talk to the girls [in the short-term program] about Christ, then when you put them together with the long-term girls, they have a different mindset which poses problems."
- "The cross is still stronger than any attempt to secularize the Teen Challenge ministry."

Some years ago, I toured in a country overseas, speaking in churches on behalf of Teen Challenge. At the end of the tour, a TC Director asked me what was different about the Teen Challenge center I led in New York compared to what I saw in the ministry he led. I replied, "We have graduates in almost every key position." He did not! Two years later, I returned to the same country and was delighted to see the indigenous principle had been launched in that Teen Challenge ministry.

We have tried to model what Paul challenged young Timothy to do: "You therefore, my son, be strong in the grace that is in Christ Jesus. And the things that you have heard from me among many witnesses, commit these to faithful men who will be able to teach others also" (2 Timothy 2:1,2).

Catherine Booth, cofounder of the Salvation Army, is quoted as saying, "A barracks is meant to be a place where real soldiers were to be fed and equipped for war, not a place to settle down in or as a comfortable snuggery in which to enjoy ourselves. I hope that if ever they, our soldiers, do settle down God will burn their barracks over their heads!"[12]

Recently a TC graduate posted on Facebook the following quote: "The cross of Jesus Christ is the reason I am alive. For His blood has set me free. It will never lose its power for me."

FOUR

WE ARE NOT PROFESSIONALS

"The Call is the inner motive of having been
gripped by God—spoilt for every aim in life
saving that of disciplining men to Jesus."

—Oswald Chambers

One of the outstanding books I have read over the last decade is by John Piper titled *Brothers, We Are Not Professionals*. The book begins with the following statement: "The mentality of the professional is not the mentality of the prophet. It is not the mentality of the slave of Christ. Professionalism has nothing to do with the essence and heart of the Christian ministry."[13]

When it comes to dealing with addiction problems, the professionals have had a go at treatment for decades often resulting in disappointment or failure. During this time, Teen

Challenge—without relying on secular professionals—has quietly been going about its work with addicts seeing them cured. Piper goes on to write, "The more professional we long to be, the more spiritual death we will leave in our wake. For there is no professional Christlikeness (Matt. 18:3); there is no professional tenderheartedness (Eph. 4:32); and there is no professional panting after God (Ps. 42:1)."[14]

This in no way justifies ignorance and the promotion of the unlearned and uneducated into positions of leadership or ministry on any level. Not in the least! However, there is a specific education that comes from living a street life, a drug life, or being an outcast that gives the set-free addict unique qualifications to identify with other addicts' pain, problems, and pressures in a faith-based rehab program. (Alcoholics Anonymous is one of the most successful programs for recovering alcoholics without using "professionals.") I had to learn through years of working alongside addicts what their mentality and struggles were in overcoming addiction. The new-born, delivered ex-addict always has an insider's view of addiction that I can never have. However, as I told one new student when he challenged me regarding my qualifications to help him, I said, "I may not be able to fully identify with your past, but I certainly am a role model for your future. I may not fully know where you've come from, but I can lead you to where you need to go."

It never ceases to amaze me as I watch those who come through our doors strung out, physically burned out, and confused make the decision to seek help only because of pressure from their family or other factors. Then, often slowly, even sometimes rebelliously, they open the door of their heart to

God—sometimes just a crack—but enough to know His love for them. The more they surrender to God, the more they begin to change. Then fast forward six, ten months after being in the Word of God, in prayer, in worship, in morning devotions, and in the care of non-professionals, and they begin to qualify as one of those non-professionals themselves. Some relapse but then seek restoration. As new disciples, they qualify to help the newcomers coming through the door who reflect what they once were. And they see, by comparison, just how far they have come due to the transformation they have received from surrendering their lives to Jesus Christ.

Is there no place in a faith-based ministry for trained counselors and what might be called "professionals" in the field of drug treatment? There certainly is. Those who have a strong biblical foundation upon which their training functions can help identify issues in a student's life that the untrained staff member may not address. I see it as faith and works functioning together. Just as a mechanic can see where a problem in an automobile engine originates, so can those who understand and identify underlying issues in an individual struggling in a faith-based program. The difference is that the mechanic knows how to correct the problem; neither a trained nor an untrained counselor can fix spiritual or emotional issues—Christ alone is the healer.

Once the indigenous workers—transformed from an addiction background—are replaced with professionals, Teen Challenge will become a secularized business. Julie Klose (my daughter), in her book *Giving Hope an Address*, quotes Randy and Pat Larson, Brooklyn Teen Challenge leaders in its early days:

Randy was often asked how he could work with addicts when he never used drugs or was an alcoholic. "It was always the issue of love for me," Randy stated. "Love for God and love for the people who walked through that door. It's not any more complicated than that." Pat added, "In our minds, we were the professionals. We were the God professionals. Every day was so exciting to see what God was going to do because something great was always happening in the lives of the students in the program. Prayer was our one tool, and if we didn't use the tool—we had nothing."[15]

In other words, if the professional becomes the substitute for the work of the Holy Spirit, and therapy or the so-called professional's role in the ministry is elevated above the work of the Spirit of God, then the gospel is relegated to either a lesser place or no place.

John Piper writes:

The professionalization of the ministry is a constant threat to the offense of the gospel. It is a threat to the profoundly spiritual nature of our work. I have seen it often: the love of professionalism (parity among the world's professionals) kills a man's belief that he is sent by God to save people from hell and to make them Christ-exalting, spiritual aliens in the world. The world sets the agenda of the professional man; God sets the agenda of the spiritual man.[16]

The experience of many people who came alongside my brother and me in the early days still applies today—or I should say, *should* still apply today; that is, many workers had no experience in drug addiction rehabilitation, but they were willing to be used by God.

> Don [Wilkerson] would often receive criticism of the program's lack of trained professionals in the field of drug addiction treatment. It was true Teen Challenge did not employ doctors or psychiatrists trained in drug recovery methods…"Our rebuttal [as staff] is that we have found that hours of prayer have been much more beneficial to our patients [students] than hours of therapy treatment… We know that whatever success we have had…has come through the power of God. Hospitals and other centers for treating addicts have failed to recognize the most important dimension of the people they are dealing with—their spiritual lives."[17]

A board member of a certain Teen Challenge once asked me, "When are you going to get more professional trained staff working with the students?" I answered, "Why don't you come and observe for yourself our ministry. Our workers are God-professionals."

Once in the early days of the ministry, the New York City mayor's office called and asked how many professionals we had on staff. My mother had answered the call but turned the phone over to me. She heard me say the number "three." After I hung up the phone, she asked me, "Who are the three professionals on our staff?" I said, "Me, David, and you. We have the Father, Son, and Holy Spirit. You can't get any more professional than that." My mother said, "I can't argue with that!"

I never apologize for our indigenous workers lacking "professional" credentials. Alcoholics Anonymous is a peer-to-peer, small group that uses successful AA members living soberly to help others be accountable. As a result, AA has success with alcoholics in the Twelve-Step program that speaks of a higher power with no definition of that power. How much more then can we have success when we identify *the* Higher Power centered on Jesus Christ.

Rehabilitation in its simplest form is one disciple showing another convert (or potential convert) what it means to follow Christ by example through word and deed: by loving others, and by deliberately doing good to the one who needs discipling. It does not take a licensed certification to do this, and, as Mark Dever put it in his book *Discipling*, it "does not begin with something we *do*. It begins with something Christ *did*."[18]

FIVE

CALLED OR HIRED

"No experience on earth is sufficient to be taken
as a call of God; you must know that the call is from God
for whom you care more than for all your experiences;
then nothing can daunt you."

—Oswald Chambers

Cross proclaimers are those who accept Jesus Christ as their personal Savior and are now His witnesses, some of whom feel called to become workers on behalf of the cross of Christ. Paul writes, "You also are the called of Jesus Christ" (Romans 1:6), which is a general call for all believers in Christ Jesus. Yet there is also a specific call to ministry like the call given to the twelve disciples who became apostles of Jesus.

No one can say that David Wilkerson went to New York to help some gang members on trial for murder simply because he was curious to learn about gangs, or because he felt adventurous in wanting to go to the gang trial. David was not curious—he was called. The call at first seemed to be a total failure, but his second trip to New York City gave him some evidence that it was indeed God who sent him to "help those boys."[19] He did all this without a sociology or psychology degree, and he was a country preacher, not streetwise. The call was birthed after days and weeks of prayer.

My own call came via telephone from my brother, sort of like the Macedonian call to "come...and help" (Acts 16:9). It doesn't matter how the call comes; it matters how it's answered. For David and me, our Pentecostal roots helped to make it clear that no one would naturally venture into pioneering a ministry to addicts without the call of God (see the chapter titled "The Call" in *Giving Hope an Address*). The call is what distinguishes those who follow God's will. Not because they are necessarily jumping with joy to obey God, but because they know they must do it as a divine assignment. It is the call that carries the called thorough the dark, uncertain times of living out that calling or mission. One's security is in the call. Paul confirms:

> Such is the confidence and steadfast reliance and absolute trust that we have through Christ toward God. Not that we are sufficiently qualified in ourselves to claim anything as coming from us, but our sufficiency and qualifications come from God. He has qualified us [making us sufficient] as ministers of a new covenant [of salvation through Christ], not of the letter [of a written code] but of the Spirit...
>
> (2 Corinthians 3:4–6, AMP)

Another way to say this is that those who are called make God their source. I learned early on in Teen Challenge ministry that neither my brother nor the board of directors were my security—only God was and is because of the certainty of my calling. The called always know that God will supply all their needs according to His riches in Christ Jesus (Philippians 4:19). My father, a pastor, taught that God always makes a way for a praying man or woman called by God.

There is a difference between someone hired as a professional and one receiving a divine calling when going into ministry. The cross is about sacrifice, and those who are asked to take up their own cross to serve in ministry make sacrifices without complaint or restraint. The sacrifices and rewards in Teen Challenge ministry include many factors: long hours, tremendous highs when students complete the program, lows when having worked with a student for months and he or she leaves the program, news of a graduate overdosing, and the constant financial struggles either in the ministry or personally, or both. Even with these experiences, the called hang in there when others quit. They receive their reward in the calling itself, regardless of the results. The called do not forsake their post, just as good soldiers would not abandon their place of duty. Professionals are hired because of their profession. The called see work in the ministry as more than a profession; it is a calling to a higher purpose by a Higher Power. I call them "lifters."

In the yearbook of my graduating class at Eastern Bible Institute, I had to write down a favorite verse. It was 1 Thessalonians 5:24: "Faithful is he that calleth you, who also will do it" (KJV). It is still one of my favorite Scripture verses and answers the question of *Who* enables the called to be successful in their calling.

A ministry built on those who feel called usually will have lower turnover of workers than an organization or ministry with mostly hired staff. For those hired, the main factor in whether they stay is the salary, but the called staff will remain regardless of the wage or even in spite of it. They also are not clock watchers.

I recall bringing an individual onto our staff with the skill and training we needed in our administrative department. This person had both the professional qualifications and evidence of the call to our ministry. For years, this call was demonstrated in accepting his position despite not being paid comparable to the same position in the secular business world. But then, for some reason, this individual wanted to be paid according to his skillset. The change in attitude, work ethic, and in other ways, was remarkable and disappointing.

Oswald Chambers writes, "The call of God only becomes clear as we obey, never as we weigh the *pros* and *cons* to reason it out."[20] No other experience or position in life can match the call of God. We know the call is from Him and not motivated by natural things, but from God for whom you care more than any other reason to serve. The called are undaunted by hardships—they always press on by the God-pressure they feel within them, knowing they must do what He wants them to do.

The called are often "lifers," in that they are in the ministry for the long haul. When someone would seek an interview with me to inquire about working with us, I would often try to talk them out of applying for a position. One such person asked me, "It seems you don't want me to work here; are you trying to talk me out of it?" She kept insisting she felt this is where the Lord wanted her. Finally, I said, "The reason I tried to talk you out of this is that if I could have [talked you out of it], I'd have known you weren't called to it—so now I know you're called by your perseverance."

Oswald Chambers writes, "One man or woman called to God is worth a hundred who have elected to work for God."[21] I'll take one called man or woman for ten or more hired ones. I have had both. Many who chose to work in our ministry did so with distinction. However, those who were called always had something extra in their commitment. Charles Spurgeon tells an interesting and humorous story about God's call:

> The general call of the gospel is like the common "cluck" of the hen which she is always giving when her chickens are around her. But if there is any danger impending, then she gives a very peculiar call—quite different from the ordinary one—and the little chicks come running as fast as they can and hide for safety under her wings! That is the call we need—God's peculiar and effectual call to His own![22]

Piper adds to this notion of ministry calling:

> What is God looking for in the world? Assistants? No. The gospel is not a help-wanted ad. It is a help-available ad. Nor is the call to Christian service a help-wanted ad. God is not looking for people to work for Him but people who will let Him work mightily in and through them: "The eyes

of the LORD run to and fro throughout the whole earth, to give strong support to those whose heart is blameless toward him" (2 Chron. 16:9). God is not a scout looking for the first draft choices to help His team win. He is an unstoppable fullback ready to take the ball and run touchdowns for anyone who trusts Him to win the game.[23]

SIX

LOVE NEEDS AN ADDRESS

"If you accuse, accuse from love. If you correct, correct from love.
If you spare, spare from love. Let love be rooted deep in you,
and only good can grow from it."

—St. Augustine

Hope and love need the same address for those seeking help. Since the first Teen Challenge opened its doors, every addict or alcoholic, or anyone with a life-controlling problem, who came through Teen Challenge should be assured they would learn that Jesus can change their life. Hopefully, on a daily basis, the newcomer will find love. Love that flows from God to each worker, and in turn, flows to those they are called to serve. A new resident was asked how he felt during the first days in the program. He said, "I felt accepted and loved. At first, I wondered, what was their angle? Then I came to realize the love was real."

One visitor who thought we might be manipulating our residents to become Christians asked a student how he was treated when he entered Teen Challenge. He answered, "They just loved me."

Love is often expressed in intangible ways: living in an environment of acceptance, not being treated like an addict but as a brother or sister in Christ—even before accepting Christ. Sometimes, all it takes to show love is a smile, a hug, or a brief word of encouragement.

The tangible ways of expressing love by the staff include sharing daily the love of God in Christ by listening to, praying with, and encouraging students, creating a general atmosphere of love, acceptance, and discipline (tough love).

From my experience, many of those who come to us for help have been in other treatment programs that focused on the problem of addiction but not on a solution. On day one in Teen Challenge in the entry process (in addition to the rules being explained), individuals are prayed for, and the power of Jesus Christ is shared with them. I'm always blessed when I've passed by our Intake Office and seen our Intake Coordinator praying for a new student coming into the program. From then on, every resident begins their day with devotions in the chapel or the devotional room. Their days in the program are in one way or another Christ-centered. This means being in a love-centered environment.

I can't say enough about the importance of a 24/7 loving, caring environment—a home away from home and, in some cases, a feeling of home some have never had. Some might call this creating a culture of acceptance and love, such as a child might experience from loving and caring parents. However, some students test a staff member's love and patience, as when they act out. At such times, love needs to get tough. Loving discipline is an integral part of the program.

One of the Scripture verses that impacted me, at about five years of working in TC, is 1 Corinthians 4:15. Paul said, "For though you might have ten thousand instructors in Christ, yet you do not have many fathers." When I read that, I was still in my twenties, and I thought, *How can I be a "father" to the young men in the program or to those who are much older than me?*

I got my answer in an unexpected way when I casually asked one of the older students how he was adjusting to the program. He said he was not doing so well. When I asked why, he said, "Because I have to take orders from you, and you're just a kid." I answered, "In this place, we don't just judge by one's biological age but by spiritual age. So, I'm actually a lot older than you; and besides, you haven't even been born yet, spiritually." He smiled and said, "Pastor, you got me there!" From then on, I knew I fit into the ministry. I would become a spiritual father to sons and daughters in the faith. What do fathers do? They love their children. It takes an alabaster box of oil in the form of a caring person showing love in tangible ways. Manifesting both tender and tough love can best be done by born-again Christians sharing the love of God residing within them as the highest qualification for ministry.

Charles Spurgeon preached, "Say not 'Our Father,' and then look upon thy brethren with a sneer or a frown. I beseech thee, live like a brother, and act like a brother."[24] The best example of love for men and women is Jesus Christ, and the mainspring of His love for people was His love for God the Father.

During Jesus' itinerant ministry, He had no place to lay His head. However, the closest thing to a home was that of Mary, Martha, and Lazarus. Oh, how He loved the two sisters and their brother. There are only two times it is recorded that Jesus wept. He did so over the city of Jerusalem (Luke 19:41), and when Lazarus died. Jesus wept over the grief the sisters experienced. John 11:35,36 says, "Jesus wept. Then the Jews said, 'See how He loved him!'" This is evidence of Jesus' humanity.

Likewise, we minister best out of a heart of love. Love is expressed in practical ways by creating in Teen Challenge a family-type atmosphere in which the residents are ministered to with respect, dignity, grace, and structure. Jesus demonstrated for Lazarus—as He does for all of us—His highest expression of love through His death on the cross. If residents are treated as "clients," then the atmosphere is less relational.

The most important point in the story of *The Cross and the Switchblade* is when David Wilkerson was rejected by Nicky Cruz of the Mau Mau gang, and he said, "You could cut me in a thousand pieces and lay them out in the street and every piece would love you."[25]

It's hard to resist love!

It does not take a professionally trained worker to love another person. One of the easiest things for gospel workers to do is connect with those they work with: a smile, a hug, brief words of encouragement, an offer to pray with the person, and so on. Some don't, but those who do reveal the reality of Jesus. People may not remember how talented we are as counselors, but they will never forget how we made them feel.

I participated in the graduation of a certain faith-based rehabilitation program. Six to eight students graduated, and as they were given a certificate of completion each graduate was asked to share their testimony. They each expressed their gratitude toward their fellow students for encouraging them during the program. But what struck me as sad is that not one of them mentioned the impact of the staff or leaders in the program. First Corinthians 13 came to my mind at that moment. Without the love of Christ displayed by loving leaders and staff, it cannot be called a true Christ-centered, love-centered program. It should not be labeled a faith-based program, nor should it carry the name Teen Challenge or Adult and Teen Challenge.

One of the most loving things I can do is tell someone they are loved by God, and if even a day goes by in which a student does not hear about such love in song, Scripture, prayer, classroom teaching, or preaching, then I am not a true servant of the Lord. This is why my heart is so heavy to know that even a single Teen Challenge is choosing to stay silent, due to certain government requirements, when it comes to ministering daily the love of God in Christ Jesus to our residents. If, as a physician, I have a medicine bottle containing a cure for some disease, and I keep it locked up, I would effectively be committing malpractice. Physicians of the soul must never keep Jesus, the Great Physician, from performing His healing.

Jeremiah 8:22 says, "Is there no balm in Gilead, is there no physician there? Why then is there no recovery for the health of the daughter of my people?" Jeremiah 46:11 parallels this: "Go up to Gilead and take balm...In vain you will use many medicines; you shall not be cured." Jesus is often referred to as the "balm of Gilead," speaking of the healing power of God's love. We are shaped and fashioned by those who love us.

My brother's vision that became Teen Challenge was to "give hope an address" (the title of Julie Klose's book), but also to create a place "so charged with this same renewing love...that to walk inside would be to know that something was afoot... It would be an induction center, where they were prepared for the life of the spirit."[26]

SEVEN

IT'S NOT REHAB

*"Teen Challenge is best understood in the
following statement: It's not rehab, it's ministry."*

—Mike Zello, Jr., President of
Teen Challenge North Central Virginia Inc.

We use the term "rehab" (short for rehabilitation) in regard to our work, just as we refer to the discipleship process as being rehab or "in recovery." Teen Challenge has used both terms *rehab* and *recovery* to help people in the secular world understand who we are and what we do. Yet, in truth, we are not a rehab program in the strictest sense of how the word is used.

I know firsthand, working at our center in Brooklyn, that many of the addicts who have come through our doors had been in short-term secular programs. A high percentage of people come to us because they have already tried other non-faith-based programs. In some cases, they were in and out numerous times with no success, and were certainly not drug-free. This motivated many to try God's way to find a cure. What if they came to us after failed attempts at rehab and were told they needed to go through a thirty- to sixty-day non-faith-based program *again*? What message does that convey to the addict? "Hope deferred makes the heart sick" (Proverbs 13:12). Hope deferred thirty, sixty, even ninety days can make the heart even sicker.

If the program is not rehab, then what are we, or what should we be?

Teen Challenge, first and foremost, is a discipleship program. We are endeavoring to make disciples of Jesus Christ like the first chosen disciples who followed Him. It is in becoming disciples that residents overcome addiction and become, according to 2 Corinthians 5:17, "new creations" in Christ Jesus. However, most who come to us do not do so to become disciples of Jesus; they come to get off drugs. Some even come just to please parents or a spouse and with no intention of serving God. The challenge then is like that of a church trying to reach the non-churched. However, because we have residents 24/7, it is easier to lay out gospel truths because we provide the time and opportunity to do so. Residents soon come to understand that in surrendering to Christ freedom from addiction is found.

Like when anyone accepts the gift of salvation, it is just the beginning of a process of seeking conformity to the life of Christ, which is known theologically as *sanctification*. Many people never move on spiritually after making the initial decision to accept Christ, showing they have not truly repented and surrendered their life to Christ. For those fighting Satan's grip of addiction, this process of discipleship is essential to long-term recovery. If we just had our residents making a profession of faith without discipleship, our results would plummet, and the students would remain in an endless cycle of relapse. We endeavor to have our staff and interns practice Hebrews 10:24,25: "Let us consider how we may spur one another on toward love and good deeds, not giving up meeting together, as some are in the habit of doing, but encouraging one another—and all the more as you see the Day approaching" (NIV). In the traditional Teen Challenge program, it is the daily example of students who are following Christ who become a continuing example and inspiration to new students to also follow Him.

So then, what the Bible calls discipleship, in the field of drug treatment we call rehabilitation. Non-faith-based rehabilitation treatment falls short of what is necessary to experience an addiction cure. This is why, in Teen Challenge, we do not say we do *rehab*. We do *ministry*. We minister Christ, not therapy. If traditional treatment is offered in TC by a psychologist or licensed counselor, it should be as a part of discipleship and not divorced from it. If such counseling is turned into a treatment program, not a discipleship program, then the program has drifted from the mission of TC. The government may pay a rehab program to offer drug treatment and therapy, but it won't pay for discipleship ministry.

Often when speaking to TC students, I tell them, "We're not here to help you get your life back. If you get it back, you'll probably mess it up again. We're here to help you give your life away—to God. Only He can change an addict from failure to success."

God makes the new man or woman, but we have to do the work of making disciples in accordance with Christ's command to "Go therefore and make disciples of all the nations, baptizing them…, teaching them to observe all things that I have commanded you" (Matthew 28:19,20). That is what discipleship is all about. Jesus said this is our job assignment. Christ does the saving; we are to do the teaching and provide the spiritual tools that help make them disciples.

Mark Dever, in his excellent book titled *Discipling*, defines the meaning of the word as "helping others follow Jesus. Discipling is a relationship in which we seek to do spiritual good for someone by initiating, teaching, correcting, modeling, loving, humbling ourselves, counseling, and influencing."[27] Any born-again Christian is capable then of being a discipler.

In this respect, discipling in its simplest form is learning "how to help others follow Jesus," which is the subtitle to Dever's book. The faith-based work of Teen Challenge in its simplest form is discipling and helping others as they follow Christ. Paul wrote that he made himself "an example of how you should follow us" (2 Thessalonians 3:9). Disciples disciple! One does not need to have a seminary education or attend a dozen seminars to disciple.

The sooner the process of discipleship begins, the sooner the healing of recovery takes place. Many try to shorten the process. But over the years, we've found that the longer the student stays in the discipleship program, the greater the results. My personal experience has been that those who enter a short-term program, whether under Teen Challenge or not, have a short-term mentality regarding wanting help. Those who go into a faith-based program know the difference between what is faith-based and what is not. They are the better candidates for lasting change.

Despite the miraculous transformation of Saul of Tarsus into Paul the missionary, after his encounter with Christ, he still needed to spend a whole year in Antioch before the church elders commissioned him for the work God called him to (Acts 11:25,26; 13:2). That year for Paul we might say was a part of his discipleship process. It takes time, as it does for all disciples.

Three important things need to take place in discipleship: repentance, surrender, and discipline.

1. Repentance. Repentance acknowledges that the root cause of addiction is not drugs or alcohol, but the deeper problem of rebellion against God or, as the Bible calls it, sin. Repentance, in its simplest form, is to turn away from living a self-centered life of sin and turn one's life over to God. Addiction is the ultimate choice of self-gratification. Repentance is the ultimate choice of sacrificing self. In the former, one gives control to a substance; in the latter, one offers control to Someone greater than himself. David Wilkerson wrote, "Come boldly to His throne of grace—even when you have sinned and failed. He forgives—instantly—those who repent with godly sorrow."[28]

2. Surrender. To some, surrender sounds like a soldier being taken into captivity, or like God wants to keep us from enjoying certain things desired in life. But surrender to God, in Christ, is surrender to a Friend who wants to give us a life better than what we have ever had before: "old things have passed away; behold, all things have become new" (2 Corinthians 5:17).

The surrender God asks of us refers to trading sorrows for joy, defeat for victory, sin for forgiveness, and hell for heaven.

Nowhere does God ask us to surrender to His will just for the sake of giving up stuff. He wants full surrender for the sake of the most important thing worth having—life in Himself.

3. Discipline. Discipline involves being committed to daily Christian practices of prayer, meditation, reading, studying the Word, and being a part of the faith community. In this respect, discipleship requires self-discipline and self-motivation to follow daily Christian practices. The "practices" are required in the program, but they ultimately need to become a habit—a new and different addiction—as part of one's future outside the program. Those who become true disciples of Christ experience that "old things have passed away..., all things have become new." Rehab, on the other hand, is short-term practice with at best a short-term success.

Being a disciple is about having a vertical relationship with Christ, but it also involves an outward horizontal relationship with authority. Being a part of the community of faith in Teen Challenge also requires imposed discipline (such as denying certain privileges) for not following program rules, disobedience to authority, and not respecting fellow students. The most uncaring, unloving thing that can be done for addicts needing new life is not telling them the truth of God's Word and the truth about themselves. Confronting with love is one of the essentials in ministering to the lost. I tell students, "The worst thing we can do to you when you leave TC is to send you out as the same person you were when you came to us. We can't let that happen and stay true to our calling and purpose."

When addicts come to Christ and make a commitment, they have to be even more vigilant in their walk than others. They have temptations that can be life-destroying. This is why they need to be supplied with spiritual weapons on day one by entering a faith-based program. With this in mind, if a faith-based program does not provide new students the opportunity to meet and accept Christ starting on day one and throughout their stay in the program—through daily prayer, worship, biblical teaching, and counseling, being surrounded with peers and staff who are following on the same path—then such a program should not be called Teen Challenge.

Again, government-funded programs are rehab, not ministry. At a Teen Challenge program, taking such funds is often justified because short-term residents are given the option to voluntarily attend a chapel service (if the state allows it). Then, following the short-term thirty- or sixty-day stay in the secular rehab, they can choose to enter the traditional faith-based program. But this is like delaying medical care to sick patients by requiring them to go through a month or two waiting period.

It seems inconceivable that an addict would be asked to enroll in a non-faith-based program to qualify for entry into a faith-based program. There is an immediacy to the gospel message, especially for an addict feeling desperate to find a cure. It is unconscionable for a faith-based program to not offer prayer and the opportunity to follow Christ on day one to someone entering a program, just so that funds can be collected each day for thirty or sixty days. That's rehab, not redemption. It is billable hours, not hours spent in God's presence.

The following quote highlights the founding vision for Teen Challenge from its beginning to now:

People [had] beaten a path to the doors of the program seeking help: the rich and the poor, the prostitutes, the drug-pushers, the strung-out addicts, the sick and the lonely. Men and women from all nationalities and various backgrounds were overcoming their life-controlling problems in choosing to follow Jesus Christ. Each new address of Teen Challenge was meeting human need by offering freedom from drug addiction.[29]

EIGHT

GETTING TO THE ROOT

"You can't endure in bearing fruit if you sever the root."

—William Wilberforce

If Teen Challenge is defined merely as a drug treatment program for addiction rather than as a Christ-centered ministry helping addicts find freedom from addiction, then it surrenders its historical mission to something the founders never intended. Discipleship/rehabilitation does not begin with something we do; it starts with something Christ did.

Years ago, I informed the New York State Drug and Alcohol Agency that we "don't work with drug addicts." Was that true? Yes and no!

At one point, some years back, we were asked to register with the State of New York as a Drug Treatment Center. I refused to do so, contending that we are a church (Brooklyn Teen Challenge is incorporated as a church) that offers spiritual therapy and Christian education for those who happen to be chronic drug and alcohol users. The state representative countered, "But you advertise as a drug treatment center?" I wrote back, "Yes, but as soon as they come through our doors, they are 'parishioners'—members of a church—who are given spiritual counsel and Bible classes. We are a church that happens to welcome addicts into our congregation. They are sinners in need of a Savior." The state left us alone after this.

Do we or don't we work with drug addicts?

Answering this question from a faith-based perspective, we are not primarily a drug treatment program. We are a discipleship program helping those with life-controlling problems to become free from the substances that control their lives, that rob them of their freedom to be a whole and a complete person made in the image of God. The truth is we talk very little about drug addiction in the classes and in messages preached in chapel services. Instead, we seek to bring our residents and congregants, those whose problems are rooted in their sin and separation from God, to salvation and a transformed life through Jesus Christ.

Addicts are not sinners because they use drugs, but they use drugs because they are sinners separated from God. Their sin causes the addiction in the same way the Bible speaks of sin as the root of "adultery, fornication, uncleanness, lewdness, idolatry, sorcery, hatred, contentions, jealousies, outbursts of wrath, selfish ambitions, dissensions, heresies, envy, murders, drunkenness, revelries, and the like..." (Galatians 5:19–21). Paul calls these "the works of the flesh"—and no one is excluded from being a sinner in need of a Savior. That is why a person who ceases using drugs still needs to be saved by God's grace. At times I tell our Teen Challenge congregation, "If you were a bunch of successful Wall Streeters I would preach to you the same basic message: 'without Jesus Christ, you are lost, but in Christ, you have eternal life.'" There is not one gospel for the addict and a different one for the successful person. Everyone must come to Christ by way of the cross.

In secular and government-funded programs, clients must be identified as "addicts" (to receive funding) and, in some cases, because addiction is defined as a disease, it is considered a disease from which there is no cure. There is, however, a cure for sin. The cure begins at the cross.

Why is the message of the cross so important in dealing with addiction? Answering this question cuts to the heart of why Teen Challenge should never be secularized. To depart from the message of the cross is to rob the addict of the delivering power of the gospel of Jesus. Then a faith-based rehab becomes just another "program" no different than the numerous government-funded treatment centers or the private programs costing thousands of dollars for therapeutic treatment.

If addiction is merely a physical craving, a disease, a habit run amok, then secular programs should work—yet they rarely do. It's incredible how simple it is to figure out what is the root of addiction. It is, first and foremost, a spiritual problem that alienates addicts from their Creator. As stated earlier, the Bible teaches that sin separates us from God. Addiction separates the addict from family, from good health, and from everyday life, but most of all, addiction separates the addict from God. Amazingly, that means the addict is not better or worse than any other human being. It is freedom from sin that is needed on the road of liberation from heroin, opioids, alcohol, or whatever drug of choice.

Four-letter words frequently heard in society are not the worst curse word uttered or heard in the streets. It's a word preachers often avoid even in churches; it's the three-letter word S-I-N. The modern reasoning that addiction is simply a disease absolves addicts from any personal responsibility for their own choices. The choice to do drugs is, first of all, rooted in the fact that men and women have a sinful nature leading to bad decisions. The disease model says addiction chooses the addict, instead of the addict choosing the addiction.

The success of faith-based rehabilitation is that it addresses this root problem of separation from our Creator-God. Often when I've asked addicts why they take drugs, they will mention a void in their lives. That void indicates the absence of God, and that absence is another way that we all "fall short of the glory of God" (Romans 3:23), which the Bible states is sin.

If there is any disease the addict has it is the fatal disease of sin. Jesus, speaking about Himself, said, "Those who are well have no need of a physician, but those who are sick" (Matthew 9:12). Sin is the sickness.

Sin made the cross necessary.

The sin problem was solved at the cross.

In the classic book by John R. W. Stott titled *The Cross of Christ*, he writes:

> Nothing reveals the gravity of sin like the cross...For if there was no way by which the righteous God could righteously forgive our unrighteousness, except that he should bear it himself in Christ, it must be serious indeed. It is only when we see this that, stripped of our self-righteousness and self-satisfaction, we are ready to put our trust in Jesus Christ as the Savior we urgently need...
>
> God could quite justly have abandoned us to our fate. He could have left us alone to reap the fruit of our wrongdoing and to perish in our sins. It is what we deserved. But he did not. Because he loved us, he came after us in Christ. He pursued us even to the desolate anguish of the cross, where he bore our sin, guilt, judgment and death. It takes a hard and stony heart to remain unmoved by love like that. It is more than love. Its proper name is "grace," which is love to the undeserving.[30]

In a faith-based program, the real program (discipleship) that frees the addict does not begin until Christ reigns in the resident's heart. And this only begins at the cross with the forgiveness of sin and the gift of salvation.

Those who run a secular, short-term program side-by-side with a traditional, faith-based program counter my reasoning by pointing out that more addicts are reached by having the short-term center. It all depends on the definition of "reached." If the short-term is just a pass-through program leading to the long-term, faith-based plan, then what is the purpose of the short-term other than financial? It is difficult for me to accept and justify that someone can enter a Teen Challenge (even if side-by-side) and not be presented with the message of the cross on day one. Yes, money is useful if the government pays per day, per resident. Still, the method is wrong even if the program operates under another entity, and yet operates in affiliation with Teen Challenge. The government-funded part is not ministry, not evangelism, not discipleship. It's the business of addiction.

So, I ask and answer the question again: "Do we or do we not work with addicts?" Yes, we do, but not strictly as "addicts." We evangelize the lost who happen to have a life-controlling problem that the Bible calls sin. To treat addiction apart from its underlying cause is to fail in providing the addict with a cure. Those who receive government funding must identify their clients as addicts but are not permitted to lead them to Christ as part of their treatment program. This means if the client leaves the program in thirty to sixty days, they have not been given the truth that can truly set them free from their addiction.

I have always considered addicts much easier to evangelize than non-addicts, because addicts have no problem admitting their life is messed up and they need forgiveness from God. Before one of our outdoor meetings in a rough neighborhood in the Bronx, I spoke to an addict who wanted me to know he had always believed in God. I asked him why, and he answered, "Look, preacher, I've had the devil in me so long I knew there had to be someone on the other side of the coin." I said, "We've come to your neighborhood to tell you about that Someone."

This is why I love working with addicts—they rarely avoid the sin question and the God-solution, unlike multitudes of others. C. S. Lewis stated: "A world of nice people, content in their own niceness, looking no further, turned away from God, would be just as desperately in need of salvation as a miserable world—and might even be more difficult to save."[31] During my years of ministry, my personal mission statement is a quote from C. T. Studd: "Some want to live within the sound of church or chapel bell; I want to run a rescue shop within a yard of hell."[32]

My daughter Julie, who I've referenced several times, wrote the following on her Facebook page:

A little history lesson on the founding of Teen Challenge:

David Wilkerson did not go to New York City to help cure drug addicts. He went because he knew there was a hurting demographic of young men and women who needed to hear the gospel of Jesus Christ—an unreached group that the church was not reaching.

But drug addiction became a symptom of those same hurting people. So, he knew you must heal the physical wounds before the spiritual. Teen Challenge, as founded, was never simply about addiction, nor should it be.

In the world of drug recovery, there are so many types of treatment programs. Drug recovery is not necessarily one-size-fits-all. I love learning about various programs that are helping those to overcome the power of addiction. Many are devoting their lives to help those with the physical wounds of addiction, and people are finding freedom.

But Teen Challenge is not solely about addiction. It's about giving people the wellspring of abundant life. That—at its core—is its identity. Over the years, it has adapted and grown, but the core identity remained intact.

Recently, those who understand Teen Challenge's core identity have seen a mission drift. Some are publicly speaking out about it to safeguard that identity. You may disagree, but I urge you first to understand the history, and from Whom its identity comes. The gospel of Jesus Christ is the lifeblood of Teen Challenge.

If there are those who want to change the identity of Teen Challenge because they don't believe in it, then simply change the name. Be a new identity in the world of drug recovery. But don't trade off a name for the sake of relevance. You don't have that right!

NINE

THE COIN IN THE FISH'S MOUTH

"For a faith-based organization, a preoccupation with financial and growth metrics unintentionally sends a message that financial and numerical successes are preeminent."

—Peter Greer and Chris Horst, *Mission Drift*

My brother started the ministry of Teen Challenge with $125.25 in the bank. Since then, finances have been an adventure, and always a faith challenge.

Jesus called Peter to be a fisher of men, and also instructed him to use the coin found in a fish to pay taxes (see Matthew 4:19; 17:27). But, if Teen Challenge residents are the fish caught in the casting net, they do not arrive with a coin in their mouth. In other words, residents in a faith-based ministry are not, or should not be, seen primarily for their financial value. Sometimes, in a fundraising appeal, I have mentioned what our monthly budget is per student, but this is to give potential donors some idea of our budget. It's also a faith goal toward our financial needs. Many traditional Teen Challenge programs do charge a modest one-time entry fee for new inductees. This in no way covers the actual monthly cost of the student. I know at Brooklyn Teen Challenge only about twenty percent can pay this fee but no one is turned away for financial reasons. The other funds necessary to cover a TC center's total budget are the result of various fundraising efforts and, especially, lots and lots of faith and prayer. I see no problem in requiring fees when the ministry remains *mission true*. A program for adolescents of necessity requires a more considerable monthly cost, as the students are limited in their fundraising efforts.

Most faith-based rehab programs operate on a shoe-string budget. I've had to live under that pressure for decades—it's both a challenge and constant testing of our faith. At times, this test caused me to engage in fundraising methods that were done not as an act of faith but out of fear and financial desperation. It is this kind of pressure over the financial budget that is behind some Teen Challenge centers' choice to seek out secular and government funding.

The faith-based way of supporting a faith-based treatment center, even with its financial shortfall, has kept the ministry alive all these years and has enabled Teen Challenge to stay true to its original mission. Miracle after miracle of financial supply has characterized most Teen Challenge ministries over the years. The reward of being faith-based is seeing God's hand in supplying the needs of the ministry. It is often used as part of the discipleship teaching to the students. I have seen the Lord use the faith and prayers of the students to supply both their personal financial needs and that of the ministry. For example, in a women's program, the ladies wanted yogurt that they did not have, and funds in the budget were tight. So, they prayed. Within days a whole truckload of Chobani yogurt was donated to the ministry—enough to last through the entire summer. This seemingly small thing became a tremendous motivation for faith in praying for even greater things.

A huge answer to prayer was shared recently when I spoke at one of our men's graduation ceremonies. One adult student, an alcoholic, entered the program having cirrhosis of the liver. During his months in the program, staff and students prayed for his healing. Before graduation, he went to the doctor for a check-up and was informed, "We can't find any evidence of cirrhosis; your liver is normal." Praying for finances is only one part of the life of faith.

Even when we have infrequently had a financial surplus, I never boasted about it but felt humbled by it and continued to be a good steward of the funds in the same manner as when finances were tight. And I certainly would not use any times of surplus to make myself look good as some big successful fundraiser. Especially if the funds came as a result of compromising what the ministry is and should stand for in respect to being Christ-centered and biblically-based. If any such funds are derived from having to compromise truth like secular treatment programs do, that's not a testimony but an indictment.

I recall one of our converts, Louis, endeavoring to open a Teen Challenge in a particular country. The cost to purchase a home for a center was about $50,000. I told him I could arrange a loan for the purchase. He said, "No, I want to pay cash for it." I kind of smiled at what I thought was his impractical faith. Then one Sunday, he spoke at a church and mentioned the financial need to buy the house. At the close of the service, when most had left the church, a man handed the speaker a check. Louis didn't look at it right away. But, as he and his wife drove away, Louis remembered the check and gave it to his wife, asking, "How much is the check?" His wife said, "$33,000." And the convert-turned-missionary taught his teacher, me, a lesson in faith and fundraising.

I do think we ought to share when God uniquely provides financial blessings. However, souls are more important than dollars. Who and what is in the student's heart is much more valuable than what is in the bank. This story, one of many, also reflects how, when souls are the priority in a faith-based program, students who graduate learn the value of God's provision and what it means to live by faith.

I confess I have looked for the miracle fish Peter found. Over the years, I had hoped one of our graduates would come from a wealth family and send us a very large financial gift. Parents are supportive and do give as they are able, but many of our residents come from low-income families and have financial challenges—so God uses other caring believers to support our ministry.

My daughter shared this personal story on her Facebook page:

I was approached about writing for a fairly large Christian ministry. Their first pitch to me was how they went from one dollar to a multi-million dollar ministry. It was impressive. I was excited. But it fell through. I remember praying about my disappointment because my writing goal is to write for Christian ministries to highlight testimonies of how God rescues and saves people through parachurch organizations. But God taught me a valuable lesson from that missed opportunity. A true ministry will pitch their worth in people's lives that have been rescued, not in financial numbers...Numbers are important. They keep your doors open. I love how God financially blesses struggling organizations who are committed to the work of the gospel. But don't let your first sales pitch be your financial status. This does not make you a ministry. It makes you a business.

We can become like Peter after the resurrection of Jesus when he said, "I am going fishing" (John 21:3). Jesus then appeared on the scene, as He had done previously when He first called Peter as a disciple. He persuaded Peter and his co-fishermen to cast their very empty nets on the other side of the boat. They did so and, as a result, gathered in a "multitude of fish" (v. 6). Jesus then invited Peter to bring "the fish which you have just caught" to Him (v. 10). Then something happened that to me appears mysterious and strange, given the context. Verse 11 says: "Simon Peter went up and dragged the net to land, full of large fish, one hundred and fifty-three..." What strikes me is that I don't think the number of fish, 153, became known by supernatural revelation either to Peter or to John, who wrote this account. If not, then how did

John know the number of fish? Apparently, Peter took the time to count them. If so, why? Jesus, the Resurrected One, was on the shore waiting for Peter to come to Him, and he was preoccupied with the number of the catch.

Each fish had some financial value when taken to market. We don't know this for sure, but Peter had decided to go back to his old profession as a commercial fisherman. He took the time to count the fish, even though he watched a miracle happen before his eyes, and the resurrected Savior was waiting for him on the shore. He did what ministries often do. Instead of finding a renewed hope in his calling or mission (which I think was what Jesus was trying to remind him of), Peter instead placed more financial value on the miracle of catching fish than the value of his primary calling as a fisher of men. This seems to be the case because Jesus then asked Peter what was most important to him: "Do you love Me more than these [fish]?" If so, feed the lambs (v. 15), not the bank account.

I grew up in the church, and my father was a denominational official. I accompanied him to many ministers' gatherings. I learned by observing that some ministers boasted about bodies and budget—members and money. I vowed not to become like that when I went into the ministry, and I pray this vow has been seen by those I have worked closely with over the years. May this be your prayer, as well.

I have a word for those leaders living with budget shortfalls. I am praying that if you stay true to walking and living by faith, you will experience the blessings of the windows of heaven poured out on your ministry (Malachi 3:10). Don't trade the red for the green (the blood of the cross for greenbacks).

TEN

TO WHOM HONOR IS DUE

"Though I am the least deserving of all God's people,
he graciously gave me the privilege of telling the Gentiles
about the endless treasures available to them in Christ."

—Ephesians 3:8 (NLT)

A visitor came into our center on one occasion and asked, "Who's in charge here?"

I don't recall who asked the question, but I'll never forget the answer from a staff member: "Sir, the Holy Spirit's in charge."

My greatest fear through the years would be that we replace the Spirit of God and become like other programs. That once birthed by the Holy Spirit, we would start to lean on the flesh. Paul expressed my fears: "Are you so foolish? Having begun in the Spirit, are you now being made perfect by the flesh?" (Galatians 3:3).

Whether our staff has theological or other degrees is not as important as whether they are filled with the Spirit and their character exhibits the fruit of the Spirit. Over the years, at our center, I found that the best staff are those who have the call, the commitment, and the compassion for our students, and most of them are graduates of the program themselves. Oswald Chambers writes, "The Christian worker must be sent; he must not elect to go."[33] We are not to choose our calling; the Caller does the calling and God chooses whom He will.

When I speak to our staff or at conferences for workers from the 1,400-plus TC programs worldwide, I often say, "You are my heroes." And they are unsung heroes at that. I note how Paul remembered so many co-laborers throughout his travels. In Romans 16 alone, he named thirty-five people who, at various times and in different churches, assisted in the work of God. They're not household biblical names, but they made Paul's list of co-laborers.

One of our graduates, Mariah, who came from a Teen Challenge women's home (The Walter Hoving Home), was asked if she wanted to work for Don Wilkerson. Her response was, "Who's Don Wilkerson?" In hiring her, it was not important that she knew who I was, but that I knew her allegiance was to the God she loved and wanted to serve. I just happened to be the one who gave her work assignments. Though she was not one of my spiritual daughters, I treated her like one.

People often come into the program broken, and according to Psalm 107:27, "at their wits' end." It's a joy to watch them, over the next weeks and months, follow the discipleship process, graduate, become an intern for a year, and then a regular staff member. This is the indigenous principle operating at its best.

One of the things I preach to new students is that I want them to leave us "redeemed, and with a résumé." The things students do in Teen Challenge include serving in community outreach, public relations, fundraising, and sales (all in the process of being witnesses for Christ). These are just a few of the experiences that help prepare them for future ministry or vocational careers. And they do this without receiving a generous salary or recognition. Nor do they do this for Teen Challenge or its leadership but for the glory of God. They are described in my daughter's book as "the God professionals."

So often, when we've had a staff position to fill, whether a teacher, mentor, cook, maintenance worker, or even a skilled carpenter, it's been a student coming through the stages of the program. We call it the "miracle in the house."

Paul downplayed the tendency even in the early church to make celebrities out of ministers. Whenever ministers, or even those they minister to, eclipse Jesus, they set themselves up in a place they do not belong. Paul reminds us, "Who then is Paul, and who is Apollos, but ministers through whom you believed, as the Lord gave each one?' (1 Corinthians 3:5). Note that effective ministers know that ministry done "through whom" and not "by whom" is what brings about growth in Christ.

Having said this, the Bible does say to give honor to whom honor is due. The kingdom of God goes forward by foot soldiers, not generals. The Bible says the first shall be last and the last first (Matthew 20:16). I've always known that on the day the Lord gives out rewards in heaven, I will be in the back of the line. Those who have been my staff, drivers, kitchen workers, computer technicians, and executive assistants will be at the head of the line. There are a lot of churches who know who David Wilkerson was and who Don Wilkerson is. Most of those who enter Teen Challenge in Brooklyn do not know who I am, and that's the way it should be.

It has been rightly said that this ministry is not about *The Cross and the Switchblade* or the Wilkerson family. What is most important is the fact that the cross of Jesus Christ is where salvation, deliverance, and changed lives begin. One advocate of the non-faith-based, short-term Teen Challenge said that partnering with the government was bringing in a "new day" for TC. To me, it is bringing in a new dark night that shuts out the light of Christ. Some have criticized my continued reference to *The Cross and the Switchblade* book as if I am making an idol of it and living in the past. One person commented to me saying, "Those who don't like to hear about your brother's book might be because the 'cross' is a challenge to their secular vision for Teen Challenge."

Those who ignore the cross do so at their own peril.

Several Adult and Teen Challenge leaders have tried to justify the government-funded program using biblical examples. One such leader tried to explain to me that this new effort was similar to when Jesus' disciples complained that outside the circle of His disciples, others were casting out demons in His name (Luke 9:49). The problem is that Jesus' name and prayer in His name are not permitted in government-funded rehabs. You cannot say you support the faith-based rehabilitation-discipleship model on the one hand and sanction the exact opposite model on the other hand.

A former staff member at one of the oldest TC long-term, faith-based programs shared how the center where he had worked changed in order to receive government funding. He said, "I watched them purge anyone affiliated with David Wilkerson and his teachings. They have put their faith in the government and their money and not God." Again, this is not about the Wilkersons' or *The Cross and the Switchblade* story; it's much deeper than that. Those who have chosen to go down the secular path have unknowingly chosen to ignore the cross. You cannot fight the cross and win!

My primary purpose here is to call attention to the traditional faith-based ministry of our organization. Those of us who oppose government funding under Teen Challenge do so because, under that name, the cross of Christ has been represented for sixty-plus years. It's been our core message. Short-term programs can be helpful for addicts who are married, have children, or are employed. However, the shorter program should be faith-based and Christ-centered just as the traditional TC model. When I have asked those who are running a secular, clinical type of program why they do so under the TC name, the answer, to my dismay, is that they want to take advantage of the success of our ministry. This is the "bait and switch" I wrote about in a previous chapter. The traditional Teen Challenge is used as the "bait" to draw people in, then "switch" them to another treatment program that is the opposite of what we have stood for since the beginning.

Having said that, I repeat that the majority of TC programs have not compromised the exclusivity of the faith-based message. Even those who do accept government-funding want every student to have an opportunity to hear and receive the message of the cross. But in my estimation, they are both promoting this and preventing it at the same time.

One of the strengths of Teen Challenge over the years is that we endeavor to follow methods that are biblical and point our students/residents to the cross. As stated previously, Greer and Horst in *Mission Drift* define those who do not depart from the founder's vision as mission true. They define these as ministries that "integrate the Gospel in all areas of their programs: There is no corner of the organizations where their Christian faith does not reach. Their products, services, policies, physical spaces, and strategies are oriented and framed by the Gospel."[34]

ELEVEN

THE BOARD OF CORRECTION

"For thus has the Lord said to me:
'Go, set a watchman, let him declare what he sees.'"

—Isaiah 21:6

Sometimes the board of directors needs to be a "board of correction" if the organization is already in the middle of *mission drift* or is heading in that direction. I view my role as that of a guardian of our ministry, and a "correction officer" when necessary. Sometimes I have done this well—and other times, unfortunately, not so well.

One time two of my board members, both close friends, came to see me. They saw something in our ministry that needed to be corrected—we were so taken up with doing in-reach rehab, as they put it, that we were neglecting outreach evangelism. My brother launched Teen Challenge with strong evangelism outreach programs: open-air street meetings, neighborhood prevention programs, coffee-house ministries, and street evangelism gospel literature blitzes. As soon as these two board members pointed out our neglect, I set in motion steps to *correct* it. Our traditional faith-based ministry always needs to be open to correction.

Over the years, there have been other problems in running a discipleship ministry, especially when using young converts in positions of leadership or using new workers from a church upbringing like myself with no knowledge about addicts or drug recovery.

One day one of the "newbies" came to see me. He and his wife were from the Midwest and fit my *calling* qualification, so they were brought into our ministry. The man's role was to be a teacher and part-time counselor to the students. One day he came to me saying he had some concerns about the program. He said, "I don't know if you are aware of it, but there are problems with the students and a few staff." I asked for an example.

He said, "The students don't listen to me when I teach."

I replied, "Yes, I understand that is often a problem here."

"Can you make them listen to me?" he asked.

I smiled and said, "No, you're going to have to earn that right on your own. Keep pressing on." I asked about other concerns he had about the program. He listed more. I smiled again and said, "Listen, the problems here are a lot worse than you know. I've been here some twenty-plus years, and you don't know the half of it."

Smiling, he said, "I guess I have a lot to learn." He did and was with us for many years.

I, too, am still learning after all these years.

Here are some of the problems of a faith-based ministry:

1. THE GALATIANS PROBLEM

My brother once made a statement that took me a few years to fully understand. He said, "The good thing about Teen Challenge is our program. The bad thing about Teen Challenge is the program." He never explained. Then the Holy Spirit helped me to interpret this wise saying from our founder. Just as the Galatians were so well-versed in the law that they thought keeping the law saved them, so too our students who work the program can come to think it is the program itself that earns them brownie points with God.

The Teen Challenge program consists of rules for behavior, Bible classes, morning devotions, prayer, homework, chores, and other work. All of those things can be done religiously, but like the Galatians who thought keeping the law was what pleased God, so too can religiously following the program be seen by TC students as the means of their salvation. Paul writes, "Does God give you the Holy Spirit and work miracles among you because you obey the law? Of course not! It is because you believe the message you heard about Christ" (Galatians 3:5, NLT).

It is the work of the cross that saves us, not the good works we do, as important as they are. Ralph Erskine stated, "I have got more hurt by my good works than my bad ones. My bad works always drove me to the Savior for mercy. My good works often kept me from him, and I began to trust in myself."[35]

Galatians 4:7 says, "Therefore you are no longer a slave but a son, and if a son, then an heir of God through Christ" (inheriting the free gift of salvation).

I wrote in my *Challenge Study Bible* the following commentary on this verse:

> Some people find security in their do's and don'ts as some-thing they can look to as an accomplishment. It is an accomplishment—but not if you follow the do's and don'ts, thinking that earns you a spiritual merit badge. Even those in programs or some type of ministry school living by rules and regulations can think that by keeping them they will be free from their problems. Keeping the rules, whether church rules, school rules, Christian practice rules (prayer, Bible reading, etc.) is good and necessary, but they're not to be followed as though you will obtain salvation by doing so. Salvation is a *gift*. What you do following your salvation is *devotion* to Christ; gratefully giving back to Him because of what He has done for you. "When a person is saved, the law moves to the side and love moves to the center... This shift from slave to son (with full rights as an heir of God) is immediate" (David Jeremiah).[36]

2. SELECTING SOMEONE FOR LEADERSHIP TOO SOON

Those I have served with over the years have an expression about me that I embrace: "God loves you, and Don Wilkerson has a plan for your life." I confess in many ways I am not a risk-taker, except when it comes to placing young men and women in places of responsibility and leadership. True, at times, my risk turns out to be a violation of 1 Timothy 5:22. However, I am still committed to helping our ministry's biological and spiritual children find their calling.

In our founding days, there were no experienced faith-based workers for rehabilitation. We had to depend on the inexperienced candidates who showed evidence of the call to our untested, fledgling ministry. My brother took a risk with me. But underlying David's telephone call to me to come and help him reach troubled youth were two things:

1. The apostle Paul's teaching that God said, "For you see your calling, brethren, that not many wise according to the flesh, not many mighty, not many noble, are called" (1 Corinthians 1:26). God chose the "foolish things" and the "weak things" of the world to put to shame the wise and powerful (1 Corinthians 1:27,28).

2. Our father strongly believed that we should "let no one despise your youth" (1 Timothy 4:12). Our father allowed David to preach his first sermon at the age of sixteen (I still remember it), and, in turn, my brother allowed me to preach my first sermon in his church when I was sixteen.

One way to kill this ministry is to prevent the young, spiritually hungry sons and daughters from being raised as leaders by replacing them with the world's professionals. We should endeavor at every opportunity to attract to our ministry young people and new converts—those willing to do God's work—if we see the gifting in them, even, and especially, when they do not see this in themselves. Some of our young leaders study online for a theological or counseling degree.

It should be on every TC's plan to be looking for what an Anglican bishop called "BWWs": Blokes Worth Watching. Every center has them, but you need a jeweler's eye to recognize a gem in the rough.

3. THE FUNDRAISING TAIL WAGGING THE DOG

Every faith-based *mission true* Teen Challenge faces financial challenges. Whether I like it or not, over the years, I have had to be a fundraiser. It takes continual faith and prayer to keep from "running out of month before running out of money." However, as pointed out previously, those whose programs receive government money are not faith-based fundraisers; they are businessmen or women.

Some Teen Challenge centers do storefront fundraising. This is when staff and students, with permission, set up a table outside supermarkets or heavily trafficked stores to share about the ministry. It is also a soft sell for funds. If done periodically, it can be a much-needed source of income, and it also enables parents and families to know a place of referral for an addicted loved one. Frequently after we've done storefront blitzes, as they are often called, our phones ring with people asking questions about the program. It also helps the students develop communication skills by sharing their testimonies (via witnessing), as well taking responsibility in their own recovery by contributing to the cost of the services they receive.

Occasionally Teen Challenges are accused of running a "work camp." I smile and say, "What's wrong with that?" I think it's unhealthy for a student to spend weeks or months in rehab with little outside contact with the public. It's important for those in recovery who might face temptations doing outside work or fundraising to do so under proper supervision. It is the ultra-liberals who want to give handouts to those unwilling to work. I could never understand private therapeutic programs and communities that keep their residents living in and confined in a therapeutic bubble—it's just not normal.

Again, I look at Alcoholics Anonymous. Those who attend their meetings leave the group sessions and may pass the same bars they used to stop in on their way to their meetings. This makes my point. Did not Jesus teach that we are to be *in* the world but not *of* the world (John 17:15,16)?

A good guideline for students doing outside work and fundraising is to do all things in moderation A good thing can become a bad thing if it becomes so successful it detracts from giving students the spiritual training and weapons they will need when they graduate.

We don't throw the baby out with the bathwater; we try to have "correction officers" in place so that fundraising becomes a means, not an end. We always try to live by this quote from A. W. Tozer: "While the world says everything by money, the church says everything by prayer."[37]

4. THE LENGTH OF THE PROGRAM

Our established policy of having a long-term program is based on years of understanding the time it takes to disciple a new believer, especially one coming out of an addiction lifestyle. The longer a student stays in the program, the higher the success rate of those who complete the prescribed program. Maturity cannot be rushed. It takes "a long obedience in the same direction," as Eugene Peterson notes in his book by that title.

Nowadays, many drug treatment programs, even faith-based ones, look for recovery shortcuts. Those who give in to it will wrong those who need long-term recovery and freedom from a life-controlling problem.

I've repeatedly seen students who start counting days or weeks of the program from their entry date. This is a big mistake, because they make time their enemy instead of their friend. There are those who are doing time and those who are doing the will of God; the former are *time slaves* and the latter are *time conquerors.* There is a short-term mentality of those seeking help from addiction. I tell students when you desire to fulfill the will of God, time ceases to be an issue. If you are a clock or calendar watcher, you will make your stay in the program more like a prison than a road to freedom.

In a church where I was speaking, a new student asked me, "How long is the program?" I thought, *Why didn't our intake person explain this?* Nevertheless, I answered him and said, "The rest of your life!" He gave me a surprised look. I explained, "I'm still in the program. Jesus is the program, and from Him you never graduate."

So, I say to those who use the program's length to justify changing the Teen Challenge program, you are going against biblical principles of discipleship, and hampering both spiritual and emotional growth, when you do so.

5. AN UNWILLINGNESS TO GIVE THE MINISTRY AWAY
My brother gave away every ministry he ever founded.

Jesus commissioned His disciples to evangelize the world. This meant that as disciples they were also disciplers commissioned to pour into others what they learned and how they were raised in the faith. If any ministry or church is to grow, it must be willing to allow others to find their place. Some church and parachurch leaders are controllers, not Great Commissioners. What I look for in a ministry's fruit is not only changed lives, but world changers raised to do "greater works" than their mentors (see John 14:12).

Only a *mission true*, faith-based ministry can give itself away. A ministry, or any part of it, that is founded or funded simply to maintain itself as a landing place instead of a launching pad is not worthy of being called anything other than a business.

My father was asked, "How does it feel to have two sons who can out-preach you?" That was not the case; nevertheless, my father said, "What kind of a father would I be not to have sons who can out-preach me?"

The sons and daughters of numerous Teen Challenge centers have gone on to be salt and light in the darkness around the world. For this reason, I do my little part to be a watchman declaring what I see (Isaiah 21:6).

I close this chapter by addressing the title of it. Yes, boards need to be both *directors* and *correctors* of a ministry, especially if they cause the *mission drift*. In the bigger picture of an organization, if the board of directors does not understand the biblical underpinnings of the organization, they can make serious mistakes and take a ministry down a slippery slope. The less a board knows of the program's history and function, the less information it will have to make the right decisions on matters brought before it. When it comes to Teen Challenge, I prefer a mixture of board members who are pastors and businessmen or women. Some boards are micromanagers and some "macromanagers." I prefer a board that is somewhere in between.

It is my experience that boards work best when they consist of men and women who don't feel the need to control the leader's agenda. Some pastors, especially denominational leaders, view the board to be top-down and may be dictatorial serving on a board. However, in the kingdom of God our mission is bottom-up in servanthood. If decisions are made without understanding the foundational mission of Teen Challenge, then this is when there is a danger of mission drift.

I have had to serve under a board all my years in ministry, and I have served on at least five boards at different times. My experience with boards has been positive, but I find most boards tend to make decisions that are financially driven. And this is why pastors on a board help keep the organization grounded in its spiritual roots.

The authors of *Mission Drift* put it best:

Mission True organizations not only hold themselves to the highest of standards because of their Christian identity, but they also recognize the contributions they are uniquely able to make to the world because of the advantages of being faith-based.[38]

I take this to heart as I have led a ministry with such a great historical tradition of saving souls and saving lives.

TWELVE

WE'VE COME THIS FAR BY FAITH

"We live from hand to mouth—from God's hand to our mouth."

—David Wilkerson

The title of the song "We've Come This Far by Faith" certainly applies to Teen Challenge. However, it's good to look at what it means to be a "faith-based" rehab organization. Primarily, it's a rehab that identifies as a Christian faith-based ministry and believes addicts are set free through the death and resurrection power of Jesus Christ, the Son of God. We also refer to it as the "Jesus Factor" in the program. This is why I have been making the case that our program's core is and should remain faith-based; the cross of Christ is and will always be central as the cure for addiction.

Calvin Miller has written, "Poets and composers may raise the Cross to the center of art and literature, but only our need and hunger can raise it to the center of our lives."[39] There is, however, another vital aspect of a faith-based ministry, and that is how funds are raised. It is either a faith effort or it uses the world's way of raising funds. The latter might involve hiring a professional firm that influences the organization to tone down its faith message to make it more appealing to non-faith donors, or to seek funds from foundations, companies, and government entities. Faith-based means it encompasses the entire ministry. The leaders need to be men and women of faith, the program's curriculum and counseling to students needs to be faith-based, and raising funds for the budget should be based on faith and prayer.

Referring again to the book *Mission Drift*, the writers point out that organizations primarily veer away from their original calling and course to chase dollars and non-faith-based donors due to changes in the board of directors. In a chapter titled "Follow the Money," the authors share the story of one international organization whose mission was to help feed children. They were experiencing declining revenue and "began soft-pedaling their Christian faith to attract new donors, but the approach did not rescue the organization." The executive director said, "We put a nice secular face on the organization."

This decision created a drift and they recognized they were heading in the wrong direction. They publicly rededicated their organization "to its roots in Christ and everything changed from that day forward."[40] When they decided to stop their *mission drift*, their annual income was $830,000. Little by little, by boldly proclaiming they were staying true to their evangelical Christian roots, their initial mustard seed faith resulted in increased donations. Nine years later, the annual revenue increased to almost $35 million.

Greer and Horst point out that according to Giving USA, in 2011, individuals and donors contributed 81 percent of charitable giving while corporations and foundations combined gave only 19 percent. The authors' maintain, "The myth [about the source of most charitable giving] drives boards of many faith-based organizations to water down their Christian distinctiveness."[41]

What are we to conclude from this? For me, I must confess that at times the residents in our program exercise more faith in God to change their lives than I have had faith in God to supply our financial needs.

My faith has never been more tested than when I have lived under the burden of meeting a monthly budget. It can lead to unwise and unbiblical decisions to raise funds. Do we partner with a secular source of funding, or do we partner with God? I've learned that faith for finances does not mean we do nothing to seek financial support; however, we must use our human efforts to meet the budget while at the same time trusting God to help us find the right sources for funds. Those sources are individual donors, churches, companies, bequests, and, surprisingly enough, from the students themselves.

I returned to Brooklyn Teen Challenge in 2008 at a time when it was facing a large financial deficit. On one of the first days in my old office, I saw an unanswered email asking if we would supply workers for two weeks to work in security at the US Open tennis matches in Queens, New York. What? Ex-cons, addicts, and former prostitutes working at a high-profile sporting event in "security"? After prayer, I saw it as a possible answer regarding our financial shortfall. Although I knew that students could possibly not be trusted to do outside work, and I also knew that some TC centers doing outside work were criticized as being a "work camp," I nevertheless saw this as an opportunity to disciple and test our students outside the bubble of Teen Challenge. The students lived up to the trust we put in them as they earned about $75,000 for the center for what turned out to be three weeks of work. We have worked for the US Open for about twelve years now, along with other area Teen Challenge programs. We have earned a combined total of 4 to 5 million dollars. The work the students do earns an hourly wage, but the funds go to Teen Challenge.

We are now sought out by both food vendors and security companies to supply the workers because of the quality of our students' work. In turn, we see this as one of the ways God provided our financial needs. Ironically, when government funds are used for rehabilitation, the residents in my estimation are unchallenged. They do not have an opportunity for spiritual growth by being tested in their faith commitment working outside in the marketplace while still being under the program's supervision. It is neither spiritually nor practically healthy that students are confined 24/7 inside what I call the "rehab bubble."

The same vendors we work with at the US Open ask us to do other high-profile events throughout the year, and we do so without the students being cheated out of the program's spiritual benefits. Work never hurts anyone, and if the only way to generate funds is through outside work—and this is seen as God's answer to a center's needs and prayers—then those who are blessed not to have to raise funds in this manner should be careful making unwise judgments about those who do.

Some Teen Challenge programs raise funds through business ventures, providing students with work experience that may help them with future job opportunities and enables them to graduate "redeemed and with a résumé." However, in using this fundraising method, the tail can wag the dog, and TCs can chase these dollars to the extent the students are overused and their spiritual development suffers. This requires good financial and spiritual oversight to make sure priorities are in order, for as Jesus said, we "cannot serve God and mammon" (Luke 16:13).

God will supply a ministry's financial needs when He is trusted to do so. The promise in the Lord's Prayer to supply our "daily bread" (Matthew 6:11) applies to organizations as well. There is something spiritually challenging in combining faith and prayer in how a ministry is maintained financially. The testimonies of how the Lord has supplied the needs for various Teen Challenges over the years are truly miraculous—I have a long, long list of such answered prayers. Strangely enough, the Scripture verse that has always encouraged me regarding the Lord supplying our financial needs is Psalm 20:7: "Some trust in chariots...; but we will remember the name of the LORD our God." This has to do with how our needs are met and who and what we are trusting in to be our financial and spiritual salvation. My brother, David, used to say, "We live from hand to mouth—from God's hand to our mouth." This may be an old-school saying for some, but the school of faith offers degrees one cannot get from any other institution.

If, by some means (and a miracle), government funding might be provided for our faith-based discipleship program, with no strings attached, we would carefully consider it. However, those funds might suddenly dry up if government policies change. The best way to utilize government funds is to provide services that most faith-based programs do not have the means to provide, such as job and vocational training, college scholarships, family counseling, and financing a halfway house to help graduates transition back into society.

Given the unlikely possibility of receiving unrestricted funds from the government, it seems we may be destined to accept things as my brother did in the founding days:

> Perhaps in this very weakness lay a kind of a power, because I knew absolutely that I could not depend upon myself. I could not fool myself into thinking that money, or high-placed connections, or a degree in sociology would be adequate to this situation, because I didn't have these things. If I were right in dreaming about a new beginning and a new environment for these boys and girls, perhaps God would choose just such a palpably ill-equipped person as I, so that the work from the very start would depend on Him alone. "Not by might, nor by power, but by my Spirit, saith the LORD of hosts."[42]

THIRTEEN

THE GOSPEL ON DAY ONE

"Do not withhold good from those to whom it is due,
when it is in the power of your hand to do so."

—Proverbs 3:27

I recall a young woman who stopped me outside our chapel and asked to speak to me. New in our Teen Challenge program, she was a businesswoman addicted to opioids. I told her I would talk to her later, but then I forgot. The next day, when I sought her out, she was gone. I never forgot that encounter with her, nor the look in her eyes when I put her off. She needed to talk to someone *at that moment*, and I never gave her that "moment." I never found out about her fate. Did she ever get the help she needed, or…? I always feel convicted when I recall this situation that took place decades ago, and it turned me into a gospel-on-day-one person.

To be worthy of the name Teen Challenge, the number-one question that every TC center should answer is this: has the gospel message been shared with a new person on *day one*? It's too easy to talk about the program and neglect talking about Jesus. Even the staff in the traditional, faith-based program can assume when a new inductee enters the program that there is time for the student to be confronted with the gospel in the days ahead and so not have an urgency to immediately encourage the person to trust in Christ or to make a recommitment on day one. We never know whether a new entry, like that woman who approached me, needs counsel, prayer, or a question answered. Those who are in need rarely tell someone they require immediate attention.

Several Scriptures convicted me as a faith-based ministry leader, especially in the days following my missed opportunity to stop and give that young woman a few moments of my time. "Do not withhold good from those to whom it is due, when it is in the power of your hand to do so. Do not say to your neighbor, 'Go, and come back, and tomorrow I will give it,' when you have it with you" (Proverbs 3:27,28). Also, 2 Corinthians 6:2: "Behold, now is the accepted time; behold, now is the day of salvation." It should always be the gospel of "now," not "later" as I was guilty of.

Many who come for help need treatment as if the Adult and Teen Challenge program is an emergency room. They are in a crisis in their addiction: possibly homeless, perhaps alienated from family, their marriage falling apart, facing criminal charges, and often physically and emotionally broken. Most understand when they enter a doctor's office that it takes time before they see the doctor. However, it should not take days or weeks to wait to be introduced to the Great Physician.

When I see Teen Challenge continue toward a mission drift, I feel like Isaiah, who wrote: "Ho! Everyone who thirsts, come to the waters; and you who have no money, come, buy and eat... without money and without price. Why do you spend money for what is not bread, and your wages for what does not satisfy? Listen carefully to Me, and eat what is good, and let your soul delight itself in abundance" (Isaiah 55:1,2).

A young man came to Brooklyn Teen Challenge from another TC program. When I asked why he left, he answered, "You can't talk about God in that place." He looked at me and said, "What do you think about this since you helped start this program?" I said, "This is not why we started Teen Challenge," hardly believing what I had just heard. He came to Brooklyn TC for two reasons: to get away from drugs and to get away from another Teen Challenge program. Who would ever believe such a thing could happen?

Some may feel that I'm too narrow-minded in my objection to the short-term programs that restrict the sharing of the gospel on day one or any other day. The residents are allowed to attend faith-based chapel services, but, still, this is not reason enough. That is like someone attending a church service without the opportunity to be a disciple of Christ. There is a great deal of difference between attending a chapel service (which is entirely optional) and being in a 24/7 faith-based atmosphere. It's true that in a faith-based TC the students are not required to accept Christ. However, chapel attendance is required, thus the possibility of conversion can happen at any given time.

My brother called Teen Challenge a "spiritual hospital," and I, in turn, am describing our intake program like an ER unit. If you have ever sat in a hospital emergency room waiting area, you may see someone with dried blood on their face, bruises, or a look of pain from some injury. In a spiritual ER, a person carries their wounds on the inside.

The two things every addict carries, whether going into a long-term or short-term program, are *guilt* and *shame*. These are the twin cripplers of addiction. As I have pointed out, an addict is not a sinner because of addiction; instead, addiction is the result of having a sinful nature. Sinners sin! There are sins associated with addiction behavior that are, at worst, criminal; other actions alienate the addict from family, friends, and society in general. All this leaves the addict with, among other things, the burden of guilt. It represents failure, a wrong, and sin on many levels. A man might have a drinking problem but continue to be a good husband, father, or professional at his job. But when he crosses a line and admittedly becomes an alcoholic and his life spins out of control, his wife and family suffer, and he may lose his job. He then adds shame to guilt, leading to more drinking to cover up the twin stalkers of guilt and shame.

Sheila Walsh, in her book *Let Go*, differentiates guilt and shame, pointing out that guilt "tells me I have done something wrong" while shame "tells me I *am* something wrong."[43] All who walk through the doors of Teen Challenge carry the sinner's guilt in contrast to many who will never admit their guilt before God or man. Paul writes, "Basically, all of us, whether insiders or outsiders, start out in identical conditions, which is to say that we all start out sinners" (Romans 3:9, MSG). I have rarely had to convince addicts that they were sinners needing God's forgiveness.

The cross represents Christ's ransom to redeem sinners of all kinds. In a Teen Challenge faith-based program, the gospel on day one holds out the possibility of forgiveness. If not on day one, it is within reach for the addict on any day and at any time. There is no waiting list, no having to serve an amount of time to have the burden of guilt lifted. It is a personal voluntary decision, not the result of staff or program pressure but the impact of the Holy Spirit's work.

The two most powerful reasons for experiencing the gospel on day one are the promises of God to set people free from guilt and shame (even if the latter comes sometime after the former):

- "Do not fear, for you will not be ashamed; neither be disgraced, for you will not be put to shame; for you will forget the shame of your youth..." (Isaiah 54:4).
- "And it shall come to pass afterward that I will pour out My Spirit on all flesh; your sons and your daughters shall prophesy, your old men shall dream dreams, your young men shall see visions" (Joel 2:28).

Joel 2:28 is connected to the previous verses that contain three promises: (1) "God...has dealt wondrously with you; and My people shall never be put to shame." (2) "I am in the midst of [My people]." (3) "I am the LORD your God...My people shall never be put to shame" (Joel 2:26,27).

Isaiah 54 challenges a barren woman to sing and shout for joy. Israel is likened to a woman without a child, a cause for shame in that day. It was a time when God's people were spiritually barren and thus living a wicked and shameful lifestyle. But the Lord was going to draw His people back to Himself with this promise: "but with great compassion I will take you back...with everlasting love I will have compassion on you" (vv. 7,8, NLT).

Nothing but the truth of God's Word can remove the twin stalkers of guilt and shame for those living in such a state of isolation from God, family, and society. If an addict is dealt with merely based on having a life-controlling problem and not on the mind and soul's deeper root problems, you may end up with a person who is drug-free but not guilt- and shame-free.

A TC graduate posted on Facebook: "To lead someone to the Lord and not follow up is to spiritually abandon them." Of course, there are times when we may share the gospel with a person and lead them to Christ as a one-time encounter with no follow-up opportunity. Addicts in a residential program, however, are a captive audience. The sooner they receive the message of the cross as the remedy for guilt and shame, the sooner they can start on the Recovery Road.

I am not trying to make a doctrine out of the *gospel on day one*, but just a point. The door into the church or a faith-based program is simply a biblical metaphor of the hope of salvation. That door brings the possibility of entering through *the* door that is Jesus Himself: "I am the door. If anyone enters by Me, he will be saved, and will go in and out and find pasture" (John 10:9). However, if there is no possibility of going through a literal door to a spiritual door, this ought to be a concern to anyone in the ministry of evangelizing the lost.

If addicts are treated just as addicts, other non-faith-based programs provide such a service. I find nowhere in Scripture the justification for withholding the truth by those who know the truth. "Hope deferred [30, 60, 90 days] makes the heart sick, but a longing fulfilled is a tree of life" (Proverbs 13:12, NIV).

AFTERWORD

While writing this book, I received an email from a person who was fired from an Adult and Teen Challenge short-term program. The offense: the former staff member prayed for a client who had an illness. From this event, I learned that the director and supervisors of these short-term programs have to police the staff in their words and actions to not violate the conditions required to receive government and insurance funds. I never thought I would see the day that a staff member was fired for prayer at Teen Challenge! The magnitude of this scenario is heartbreaking.

I've been asked what I seek to accomplish with writing this book.

First, as I have emphasized, most Adult and Teen Challenge programs have stayed *mission true*. They are discipleship ministries and not drug-treatment programs or businesses.

Secondly, I will continue to ask that those Teen Challenge centers who do not share the *gospel on day one* change their name.

Some of these programs share the history of Teen Challenge on their websites—my brother's visit to New York City to help gang members on trial for murder. The founding story of David Wilkerson and *The Cross and the Switchblade* is about a ministry birthed and rooted in prayer. Using this association is an insult to me, especially when TC staff members are dismissed because of prayer. If my brother were alive today, he would very likely ask that they remove any reference to himself and the founding story of Teen Challenge from their websites.

In one of these non-faith-based programs, the dining room is called the "Wilkerson Hall." I am ashamed to have my family name on that building, which can be seen while driving onto the Teen Challenge property.

Some have said a short-term, non-faith-based program can reach more addicts because it is side-by-side with the traditional Teen Challenge, and the clients can choose to enter the faith-based program. This is true, but my question is, why does a faithless, prayerless, gospel-less program need to be called Teen Challenge?

To make a clear distinction between the two different programs, remove the name of Teen Challenge from the secular rehab program which is, in fact, *not* what Teen Challenge has represented through the years.

Whenever I have posted about my objection to the short-term Teen Challenge programs compromising the gospel, the overwhelming feedback has been that these centers should change their name. The following sums up what most supporters of Teen Challenge have to say about this:

> You must be separate. If prayer isn't allowed, then it's not God and shouldn't be a part of Teen Challenge. Let it be a

separate secular clinic that refers clients to Teen Challenge as a hospital's detox center refers to patients.

I don't want to meet someone wearing an Adult and Teen Challenge T-shirt who went through the short-term program but was never introduced to Jesus Christ or biblically discipled. The person may be drug-free but not free in Christ. There is an eternal difference between those who have a relapse in their addiction and those who may have never been confronted with the *truth* that can set them free—from all their sins. Again, I repeat, Teen Challenge is to be primarily an *evangelism* ministry, not a drug treatment program. We should not be willing to sacrifice the ultimate good of those we serve simply for the sake of finances. All our students should be served in the name of Jesus alone. "No one can serve two masters; for either he will hate the one and love the other, or else he will be loyal to the one and despise the other. You cannot serve God and mammon" (Matthew 6:24).

NOTES

1. Peter Greer and Chris Horst, *Mission Drift: The Unspoken Crisis Facing Leaders, Charities, and Churches* (Grand Rapids, MI: Bethany House Publishers, 2014), 27.

2. Ibid., 85.

3. Ibid., 12.

4. Julie Wilkerson Klose, *Giving Hope an Address: The Teen Challenge Legacy Story* (Newberry, FL: Bridge-Logos, 2018), 61.

5. A. W. Tozer, *The Radical Cross* (Chicago: Moody Bible Institute, 2009), 15.

6. "Day One" lyrics © Kobalt Music Publishing Ltd.

7. "At the Cross" lyrics by Isaac Watts <greatchristianhymns.com/at-the-cross.html>.

8. "Power in the Blood" lyrics by Lewis E. Jones, 1899.

9. *The Complete Guide to Christian Quotations* (Uhrichsville, Ohio: Barbour Publishing, 2011), 88.

10. Greer and Horst, *Mission Drift*, 99.

11. "Indigenous," TheFreeDictionary.com <thefreedictionary.com/indigenous>.

12. AZ Quotes <azquotes.com/author/30084-Catherine_Booth>.

13. John Piper, *Brothers, We Are Not Professionals: A Plea to Pastors for Radical Ministry* (Nashville, TN: B&H Publishing Group, 2013), 1.

14. Ibid.

15. Klose, *Giving Hope an Address*, 94–95.

16. Piper, *Brothers, We Are Not Professionals*, 3.

17. Klose, *Giving Hope an Address*, 94.

18. Mark Dever, *Discipling: How to Help Others Follow Jesus* (Wheaton, IL: Crossway, 2016), 14.

19. David Wilkerson, *The Cross and the Switchblade* (New York: A Jove Book, 1962), 7.

20. Oswald Chambers, *The Best from All His Books* (Nashville, TN: Oliver-Nelson Books, 1987), 34.

21. Ibid.

22. C. H. Spurgeon, "Speak, Lord!," sermon delivered at the Metropolitan Tabernacle, Newington, March 20, 1884 <ccel.org/ccel/spurgeon/sermons43.xxix.html>.

23. Piper, *Brothers, We Are Not Professionals*, 56.

24. C. H. Spurgeon, "The Fatherhood of God," sermon delivered September 12, 1858, at the Music Hall, Royal Surrey Gardens <ccel.org/ccel/spurgeon/sermons04.xlix.html>.

25. David Wilkerson, *The Cross and the Switchblade* (Grand Rapids, MI: Chosen Books, 2008), 80.

26. Klose, *Giving Hope an Address*, 41–42.

27. Dever, *Discipling*, 74.

28. David Wilkerson, "A Dry Spell," February 1, 1979, World Challenge <worldchallenge.org/content/dry-spell>.

29. Klose, *Giving Hope an Address*, 88.

30. John R. W. Stott, *The Cross of Christ* (Downers Grove, IL: InterVarsity Press, 1986, 2006), 85.

31. C. S. Lewis, *Mere Christianity* (San Francisco: Harper Collins, 2001), 215.

32. Grace Quotes <tinyurl.com/y23rjkxt>.

33. Verploegh, *Oswald Chambers: The Best from All His Books*, 384.

34. Greer and Horst, *Mission Drift*, 146.

35. Quoted in *365 Days with C. H. Spurgeon*, Vol. 1, Terence Peter Crosby, ed. (Day One Publications, 1998).

36. Don Wilkerson, *The Challenge Study Bible* (Newberry, FL: Bridge-Logos, Inc., 2019), 1743.

37. A. W. Tozer, "In Everything by Prayer," Discipleship Library <discipleshiplibrary.com/pdfs/NET01859.pdf>.

38. Greer and Horst, *Mission Drift*, 142.

39. Calvin Miller, *Once Upon a Tree* (West Monroe, LA: Howard Publishing Co., 2002), 13.

40. Ibid., 114.

41. Ibid., 113.

42. Wilkerson, *The Cross and the Switchblade*, 72.

43. Shelia Walsh, *Let Go: Live Free of the Burdens All Women Know* (Nashville, TN: Thomas Nelson, 2008), 102.

STAYING MISSION TRUE:
THE WILKERSON LIBRARY

Beyond what has been shared in this book, the challenge now is how to remain *mission true* as a faith-focused, Christ-centered ministry. I have made a commitment in this regard by the proposed opening of the Wilkerson Library at the original Teen Challenge Men's Home at 416 Clinton Avenue, Brooklyn, New York. In spite of its name, this is not a memorial to my brother, David Wilkerson, or me. It is about what the Lord established through us over sixty years ago. The library is a place to share the historical roots and founding principles of Teen Challenge. When you understand its history, you will know which direction to take it into the future. May it always reflect 2 Corinthians 5:17: "Therefore, if anyone is in Christ, he is a new creation; old things have passed away; behold, all things have become new."

Your financial gift will help establish the Wilkerson Library. You can give an offering at:

Donwilkersononline.com

or

Brooklyntc.org

Brooklyn Teen Challenge
416 Clinton Avenue
Brooklyn, NY 11238

Please note on the check for "Wilkerson Library."